DATE DUE		
DEC 1 5 1999		

THOMAS PAINE

THOMAS PAINE

John Vail

CHELSEA HOUSE PUBLISHERS
NEW YORK
PHILADELPHIA

Chelsea House Publishers
EDITOR-IN-CHIEF: Nancy Toff
EXECUTIVE EDITOR: Remmel T. Nunn
MANAGING EDITOR: Karyn Gullen Browne
COPY CHIEF: Juliann Barbato
PICTURE EDITOR: Adrian G. Allen
ART DIRECTOR: Maria Epes
MANUFACTURING MANAGER: Gerald Levine

World Leaders—Past & Present
SENIOR EDITOR: John W. Selfridge

Staff for THOMAS PAINE
COPY EDITOR: Philip Koslow
EDITORIAL ASSISTANT: Nate Eaton
PICTURE RESEARCHER: Andrea Reithmayr
ASSISTANT ART DIRECTOR: Loraine Machlin
DESIGNER: James Baker
PRODUCTION MANAGER: Joseph Romano
PRODUCTION COORDINATOR: Marie Claire Cebrián
COVER ILLUSTRATION: Bill Donahey

3 5 7 9 8 6 4 2

Library of Congress Cataloging-in-Publication Data

Vail, John J.
  Thomas Paine/John Vail.
    p.   cm.—(World leaders past & present)
  Includes bibliographical references.
  Summary: Examines the life of the influential political writer
whose pamphlet "Common Sense" became one of the basic tracts of
the American Revolution.
  ISBN 1-55546-819-5
        0-7910-0701-4 (pbk.)
  1. Paine, Thomas. 1737–1809—Juvenile literature. 2. Political
scientists—United States—Biography—Juvenile literature.
3. Revolutionists—United States—Biography—Juvenile literature.
[1. Paine, Thomas, 1737–1809. 2. Political scientists.] I. Title.
II. Series.
JC178.V2V27   1990   89-38479
320.5′1′092—dc20   CIP
[B]   AC

Contents

John Adams
John Quincy Adams
Konrad Adenauer
Alexander the Great
Salvador Allende
Marc Antony
Corazon Aquino
Yasir Arafat
King Arthur
Hafez al-Assad
Kemal Atatürk
Attila
Clement Attlee
Augustus Caesar
Menachem Begin
David Ben-Gurion
Otto von Bismarck
Léon Blum
Simon Bolívar
Cesare Borgia
Willy Brandt
Leonid Brezhnev
Julius Caesar
John Calvin
Jimmy Carter
Fidel Castro
Catherine the Great
Charlemagne
Chiang Kai-Shek
Winston Churchill
Georges Clemenceau
Cleopatra
Constantine the Great
Hernán Cortés
Oliver Cromwell
Georges-Jacques
  Danton
Jefferson Davis
Moshe Dayan
Charles de Gaulle
Eamon De Valera
Eugene Debs
Deng Xiaoping
Benjamin Disraeli
Alexander Dubček
François & Jean-Claude
  Duvalier
Dwight Eisenhower
Eleanor of Aquitaine
Elizabeth I
Faisal
Ferdinand & Isabella
Francisco Franco
Benjamin Franklin

Frederick the Great
Indira Gandhi
Mohandas Gandhi
Giuseppe Garibaldi
Amin & Bashir Gemayel
Genghis Khan
William Gladstone
Mikhail Gorbachev
Ulysses S. Grant
Ernesto "Che" Guevara
Tenzin Gyatso
Alexander Hamilton
Dag Hammarskjöld
Henry VIII
Henry of Navarre
Paul von Hindenburg
Hirohito
Adolf Hitler
Ho Chi Minh
King Hussein
Ivan the Terrible
Andrew Jackson
James I
Wojciech Jaruzelski
Thomas Jefferson
Joan of Arc
Pope John XXIII
Pope John Paul II
Lyndon Johnson
Benito Juárez
John Kennedy
Robert Kennedy
Jomo Kenyatta
Ayatollah Khomeini
Nikita Khrushchev
Kim Il Sung
Martin Luther King, Jr.
Henry Kissinger
Kublai Khan
Lafayette
Robert E. Lee
Vladimir Lenin
Abraham Lincoln
David Lloyd George
Louis XIV
Martin Luther
Judas Maccabeus
James Madison
Nelson & Winnie
  Mandela
Mao Zedong
Ferdinand Marcos
George Marshall

Mary, Queen of Scots
Tomáš Masaryk
Golda Meir
Klemens von Metternich
James Monroe
Hosni Mubarak
Robert Mugabe
Benito Mussolini
Napoléon Bonaparte
Gamal Abdel Nasser
Jawaharlal Nehru
Nero
Nicholas II
Richard Nixon
Kwame Nkrumah
Daniel Ortega
Mohammed Reza Pahlavi
Thomas Paine
Charles Stewart
  Parnell
Pericles
Juan Perón
Peter the Great
Pol Pot
Muammar el-Qaddafi
Ronald Reagan
Cardinal Richelieu
Maximilien Robespierre
Eleanor Roosevelt
Franklin Roosevelt
Theodore Roosevelt
Anwar Sadat
Haile Selassie
Prince Sihanouk
Jan Smuts
Joseph Stalin
Sukarno
Sun Yat-sen
Tamerlane
Mother Teresa
Margaret Thatcher
Josip Broz Tito
Toussaint L'Ouverture
Leon Trotsky
Pierre Trudeau
Harry Truman
Queen Victoria
Lech Walesa
George Washington
Chaim Weizmann
Woodrow Wilson
Xerxes
Emiliano Zapata
Zhou Enlai

CHELSEA HOUSE PUBLISHERS

ON LEADERSHIP

Arthur M. Schlesinger, jr.

LEADERSHIP, it may be said, is really what makes the world go round. Love no doubt smooths the passage; but love is a private transaction between consenting adults. Leadership is a public transaction with history. The idea of leadership affirms the capacity of individuals to move, inspire, and mobilize masses of people so that they act together in pursuit of an end. Sometimes leadership serves good purposes, sometimes bad; but whether the end is benign or evil, great leaders are those men and women who leave their personal stamp on history.

Now, the very concept of leadership implies the proposition that individuals can make a difference. This proposition has never been universally accepted. From classical times to the present day, eminent thinkers have regarded individuals as no more than the agents and pawns of larger forces, whether the gods and goddesses of the ancient world or, in the modern era, race, class, nation, the dialectic, the will of the people, the spirit of the times, history itself. Against such forces, the individual dwindles into insignificance.

So contends the thesis of historical determinism. Tolstoy's great novel *War and Peace* offers a famous statement of the case. Why, Tolstoy asked, did millions of men in the Napoleonic Wars, denying their human feelings and their common sense, move back and forth across Europe slaughtering their fellows? "The war," Tolstoy answered, "was bound to happen simply because it was bound to happen." All prior history predetermined it. As for leaders, they, Tolstoy said, "are but the labels that serve to give a name to an end and, like labels, they have the least possible connection with the event." The greater the leader, "the more conspicuous the inevitability and the predestination of every act he commits." The leader, said Tolstoy, is "the slave of history."

Determinism takes many forms. Marxism is the determinism of class. Nazism the determinism of race. But the idea of men and women as the slaves of history runs athwart the deepest human instincts. Rigid determinism abolishes the idea of human freedom—

the assumption of free choice that underlies every move we make, every word we speak, every thought we think. It abolishes the idea of human responsibility, since it is manifestly unfair to reward or punish people for actions that are by definition beyond their control. No one can live consistently by any deterministic creed. The Marxist states prove this themselves by their extreme susceptibility to the cult of leadership.

More than that, history refutes the idea that individuals make no difference. In December 1931 a British politician crossing Park Avenue in New York City between 76th and 77th Streets around 10:30 P.M. looked in the wrong direction and was knocked down by an automobile—a moment, he later recalled, of a man aghast, a world aglare: "I do not understand why I was not broken like an eggshell or squashed like a gooseberry." Fourteen months later an American politician, sitting in an open car in Miami, Florida, was fired on by an assassin; the man beside him was hit. Those who believe that individuals make no difference to history might well ponder whether the next two decades would have been the same had Mario Constasino's car killed Winston Churchill in 1931 and Giuseppe Zangara's bullet killed Franklin Roosevelt in 1933. Suppose, in addition, that Adolf Hitler had been killed in the street fighting during the Munich *Putsch* of 1923 and that Lenin had died of typhus during World War I. What would the 20th century be like now?

For better or for worse, individuals do make a difference. "The notion that a people can run itself and its affairs anonymously," wrote the philosopher William James, "is now well known to be the silliest of absurdities. Mankind does nothing save through initiatives on the part of inventors, great or small, and imitation by the rest of us—these are the sole factors in human progress. Individuals of genius show the way, and set the patterns, which common people then adopt and follow."

Leadership, James suggests, means leadership in thought as well as in action. In the long run, leaders in thought may well make the greater difference to the world. But, as Woodrow Wilson once said, "Those only are leaders of men, in the general eye, who lead in action. . . . It is at their hands that new thought gets its translation into the crude language of deeds." Leaders in thought often invent in solitude and obscurity, leaving to later generations the tasks of imitation. Leaders in action—the leaders portrayed in this series—have to be effective in their own time.

And they cannot be effective by themselves. They must act in response to the rhythms of their age. Their genius must be adapted, in a phrase of William James's, "to the receptivities of the moment." Leaders are useless without followers. "There goes the mob," said the French politician hearing a clamor in the streets. "I am their leader. I must follow them." Great leaders turn the inchoate emotions of the mob to purposes of their own. They seize on the opportunities of their time, the hopes, fears, frustrations, crises, potentialities. They succeed when events have prepared the way for them, when the community is awaiting to be aroused, when they can provide the clarifying and organizing ideas. Leadership ignites the circuit between the individual and the mass and thereby alters history.

It may alter history for better or for worse. Leaders have been responsible for the most extravagant follies and most monstrous crimes that have beset suffering humanity. They have also been vital in such gains as humanity has made in individual freedom, religious and racial tolerance, social justice, and respect for human rights.

There is no sure way to tell in advance who is going to lead for good and who for evil. But a glance at the gallery of men and women in *World Leaders—Past and Present* suggests some useful tests.

One test is this: Do leaders lead by force or by persuasion? By command or by consent? Through most of history leadership was exercised by the divine right of authority. The duty of followers was to defer and to obey. "Theirs not to reason why / Theirs but to do and die." On occasion, as with the so-called enlightened despots of the 18th century in Europe, absolutist leadership was animated by humane purposes. More often, absolutism nourished the passion for domination, land, gold, and conquest and resulted in tyranny.

The great revolution of modern times has been the revolution of equality. The idea that all people should be equal in their legal condition has undermined the old structure of authority, hierarchy, and deference. The revolution of equality has had two contrary effects on the nature of leadership. For equality, as Alexis de Tocqueville pointed out in his great study *Democracy in America*, might mean equality in servitude as well as equality in freedom.

"I know of only two methods of establishing equality in the political world," Tocqueville wrote. "Rights must be given to every citizen, or none at all to anyone . . . save one, who is the master of all." There was no middle ground "between the sovereignty of all and the absolute power of one man." In his astonishing prediction of 20th-century totalitarian dictatorship, Tocqueville explained how the revolution of equality could lead to the *"Führerprinzip"* and more terrible absolutism than the world had ever known.

But when rights are given to every citizen and the sovereignty of all is established, the problem of leadership takes a new form, becomes more exacting than ever before. It is easy to issue commands and enforce them by the rope and the stake, the concentration camp and the *gulag*. It is much harder to use argument and achievement to overcome opposition and win consent. The Founding Fathers of the United States understood the difficulty. They believed that history had given them the opportunity to decide, as Alexander Hamilton wrote in the first Federalist Paper, whether men are indeed capable of basing government on "reflection and choice, or whether they are forever destined to depend . . . on accident and force."

Government by reflection and choice called for a new style of leadership and a new quality of followership. It required leaders to be responsive to popular concerns, and it required followers to be active and informed participants in the process. Democracy does not eliminate emotion from politics; sometimes it fosters demagoguery; but it is confident that, as the greatest of democratic leaders put it, you cannot fool all of the people all of the time. It measures leadership by results and retires those who overreach or falter or fail.

It is true that in the long run despots are measured by results too. But they can postpone the day of judgment, sometimes indefinitely, and in the meantime they can do infinite harm. It is also true that democracy is no guarantee of virtue and intelligence in government, for the voice of the people is not necessarily the voice of God. But democracy, by assuring the right of opposition, offers built-in resistance to the evils inherent in absolutism. As the theologian Reinhold Niebuhr summed it up, "Man's capacity for justice makes democracy possible, but man's inclination to injustice makes democracy necessary."

A second test for leadership is the end for which power is sought. When leaders have as their goal the supremacy of a master race or the promotion of totalitarian revolution or the acquisition and exploitation of colonies or the protection of greed and privilege or the preservation of personal power, it is likely that their leadership will do little to advance the cause of humanity. When their goal is the abolition of slavery, the liberation of women, the enlargement of opportunity for the poor and powerless, the extension of equal rights to racial minorities, the defense of the freedoms of expression and opposition, it is likely that their leadership will increase the sum of human liberty and welfare.

Leaders have done great harm to the world. They have also conferred great benefits. You will find both sorts in this series. Even "good" leaders must be regarded with a certain wariness. Leaders are not demigods; they put on their trousers one leg after another just like ordinary mortals. No leader is infallible, and every leader needs to be reminded of this at regular intervals. Irreverence irritates leaders but is their salvation. Unquestioning submission corrupts leaders and demeans followers. Making a cult of a leader is always a mistake. Fortunately hero worship generates its own antidote. "Every hero," said Emerson, "becomes a bore at last."

The signal benefit the great leaders confer is to embolden the rest of us to live according to our own best selves, to be active, insistent, and resolute in affirming our own sense of things. For great leaders attest to the reality of human freedom against the supposed inevitabilities of history. And they attest to the wisdom and power that may lie within the most unlikely of us, which is why Abraham Lincoln remains the supreme example of great leadership. A great leader, said Emerson, exhibits new possibilities to all humanity. "We feed on genius. . . . Great men exist that there may be greater men."

Great leaders, in short, justify themselves by emancipating and empowering their followers. So humanity struggles to master its destiny, remembering with Alexis de Tocqueville: "It is true that around every man a fatal circle is traced beyond which he cannot pass; but within the wide verge of that circle he is powerful and free; as it is with man, so with communities."

1

The Young Revolutionary

On September 13, 1792, Thomas Paine stood on the docks in Dover, England. Before him stretched the English Channel, and beyond it lay France. He glanced back one final time at his homeland and then redirected his gaze out to sea.

Seventeen years earlier, he had left England for the first time to seek his fame and fortune in the New World, America. Within two years he became one of the most celebrated literary figures in the world by virtue of his pamphlets in support of the American War of Independence. When Paine returned to England in 1787, he was quickly caught up in the wave of revolutionary fervor that was sweeping Europe at the time. In 1791, he wrote *The Rights of Man*, an impassioned defense of the French Revolution of 1789 and a denunciation of the British monarchy. The book was a huge commercial success, but in the eyes of the British government the book made Paine an enemy of the state.

Vive Thomas Paine!
—crowd in Calais, France, on the occasion of Paine's arrival in 1792

Thomas Paine believed in the essential goodness of humanity and in the citizen's right to participatory government. In his book *The Rights of Man*, Paine argued that republicanism was the best form of government and condemned the monarchical rule of France and England. Consequently, he was charged with treason.

Paine's book sparked the imagination of the nation's workers and poor people: Membership in radical political societies grew, and there emerged a widespread discontent with the British government, which began to fear that Paine's writings might inspire a revolutionary movement in England itself. For months after the publication of *The Rights of Man*, Paine was hounded by the British government. Spies followed him everywhere, his mail was opened, and his books were burned.

Paine not only refused to renounce his beliefs or apologize for his political activities, but in late August he delivered a provocative speech urging the abolition of the monarchy and the establishment of a republic in England. Although friends warned him that his arrest was imminent, Paine did not believe the government would dare risk an open trial, where he could publicly assert his position. On the day after his speech, however, his friend William Blake, the noted poet, told him: "You must not go home or you are a dead man." This time, Paine wisely heeded the advice and hurriedly left on a train to Dover, where he planned to board a ship to France. Just a few hours after his departure, bailiffs arrived at his apartment with a warrant for his arrest.

Paine chose France as his new destination because of his fervent support of the French Revolu-

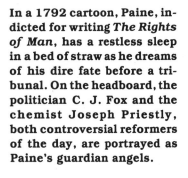

In a 1792 cartoon, Paine, indicted for writing *The Rights of Man*, has a restless sleep in a bed of straw as he dreams of his dire fate before a tribunal. On the headboard, the politician C. J. Fox and the chemist Joseph Priestly, both controversial reformers of the day, are portrayed as Paine's guardian angels.

King Louis XVI is held at bayonet point in 1792, when he was deposed and a new revolutionary government was formed in France. Paine, who rejected capital punishment as barbaric, argued passionately for the king's life to be spared.

tion. In the years since the advent of the Revolution on July 14, 1789, France had been governed by a constitutional monarchy, but in August 1792, a revolutionary insurrection in Paris deposed the king and established a new revolutionary government. In that same month, the National Assembly of France conferred honorary citizenship on 17 foreigners who "by their writings and by their courage, have served the cause of liberty and prepared the freedom of the people." Among those honored were George Washington, Alexander Hamilton, James Madison, and Thomas Paine, who was especially cited for his essays supporting the American Revolution.

During elections for the new French legislature, known as the National Convention, the region of Calais elected Paine as its deputy to this new assembly. Given the increasingly hostile atmosphere in England, Paine gladly accepted the offer.

A French peasant family gathers for a bible reading. During the reign of Louis XVI, the vast majority of French peasants and laborers paid large sums of money in taxes to the monarchy and rents to the aristocracy while they lived in abject poverty on small, barely arable plots of land.

Now, awaiting the ferry to Calais, Paine sat by stoically as British customs officials searched his luggage, examined his personal papers, and opened his private correspondence, which included a personal letter from the president of the United States, George Washington. Then, Paine's friend Achille Audibert, who had been sent from Calais to escort Paine to France, threatened to lodge a formal protest by the French government unless Paine was allowed to depart immediately with all of his possessions intact. The officials finally relented, but there was one more humiliation to bear: As Paine boarded his ship, boos and catcalls resounded from the crowd that had gathered to witness his departure.

Paine's arrival in Calais the following afternoon stood in stark contrast to his British send-off. A company of soldiers greeted him with an impressive gun salute. The officer in charge embraced Paine and presented him with a cockade — the red-white-and-blue feather that was the symbol of the Revolution. A young woman asked Paine if she could have the honor of placing it in his hat and, as she secured it firmly in place, told him that she hoped he would continue to fight for liberty and equality in France. Huge crowds gathered along the rue de l'Égalité — formerly the rue du Roi (street of the king) — to herald Paine's passage into town, shouting, "Vive Thomas Paine!" In front of the city hall, the mayor of Calais and other assembled dignitaries warmly praised his achievements, and Paine pledged that his life would henceforth be devoted to the cause of the French Revolution. "A share in two revolutions," he would later write, "is living to some purpose."

European societies of the 18th century were dominated by corrupt monarchical bureaucracies. The great majority of the rural population were peasants who farmed small, inefficient plots and paid annual dues and rents to the ruling aristocracy. Whereas the peasants and the poor lived in squalid conditions, the rich resided in palatial country estates, dressed in finery, and traveled in horse-drawn carriages. The cities, too, were characterized by rigid social hierarchies and vast disparities in wealth. Because power and privilege were reserved for the aristocracy, the church, and the bourgeoisie, those groups forcefully maintained the status quo. The peasant and the urban artisan, who had the most interest in change, had no political leverage.

The royal family of England in 1787. The corrupt monarchies that dominated 18th-century European societies enjoyed unlimited power and wealth while the masses went hungry. Paine, recognizing the plight of the common citizen, was committed to abolishing hereditary rule and replacing monarchies with republican governments.

Thomas Paine was born on January 29, 1737, in the village of Thetford, England, into a society that embodied many of these features. Although England was the only European nation that had evolved a constitutional system with a separation of powers between the monarchy and the legislature, the system in practice was, nevertheless, severely limited by class privilege. The king still exerted tremendous authority by virtue of his power to appoint and dismiss ministers and by his extensive patronage influence. Voting rights were restricted by property qualifications; in the corrupt "rotten borough" electoral system, many districts held no electoral contests at all and the overwhelming preponderance of elected representatives to Parliament came from the underpopulated rural districts.

In this William Hogarth engraving, a typical English village goes about its business on election day. Because only property owners could vote in 18th-century England, the majority of the population was disenfranchised.

England was also a predominantly rural society in the 18th century, but agricultural production was being transformed into more profitable commercial enterprises. Thousands of independent farmers, displaced from their land, were compelled either to work as laborers on others' farms or to move to the cities and become factory workers. Poverty, misery, and degradation plagued the lower classes; they were victimized by the legal system, disenfranchised from the nation's political life, and reduced to a meager existence by economic inequality.

From all appearances, European society seemed static and impervious to change. However, beneath the placid surface there were startling new intellectual forces that were bringing about a momentous transformation. The Enlightenment, as historians have termed it, began with the development of modern science in the 17th century. Scientific discoveries were premised upon a faith in the potential of human reason: the belief that the laws of nature were rational and could be discovered and comprehended by the human intellect. Modern science provided new ideas that were distinct from religious dogma and inspired new dreams of intellectual and material progress.

A kind of fungus growing out of the corruption of society . . . a sort of mule animal, capable only of destroying and not breeding up.
—THOMAS PAINE
on the aristocracy of 18th-century Europe

The advances of the sciences were matched by the accomplishments of the era's political thinkers, who believed in the innate goodness of every person, the power of human reason, and the progress of human history toward a better world. John Locke, for example, loosened the underpinnings of current political systems by asserting that political sovereignty should rest with the people, not with the monarchy, and that every government should be informed by the consent of the people. Another Enlightenment philosopher, Jean-Jacques Rousseau, argued that every citizen has inalienable individual rights and should participate fully in the nation's political affairs.

The rise of the Enlightenment coincided with the further development of the printing press and the consequent growth of Europe's literate population. As more people began to read, the ideas of the Enlightenment philosophers reached all segments of

European society. Because these ideas posed such a powerful challenge to traditional authority, they also served as a rallying point for revolutionary change. Paine and other leaders of the American and French revolutions would take up the slogans of the Enlightenment and use them to provide the foundation for a new political order in America and Europe.

Thomas Paine's parents were separated by differences in class, temperament, and religion. His father, Joseph Pain (Thomas added the *e* to his family name when he moved to America), was an easygoing Quaker who worked as a staymaker, constructing the cumbersome corsets that affluent women of the era wore underneath their dresses. Paine's mother, Frances, was 11 years older than her husband and a member of the Church of England. The daughter of a Thetford attorney, one of the village elite, she was a severe, ill-tempered woman.

Religion was the most important feature of the Paine household. Young Thomas spent many long hours studying the Bible or attending religious instruction. Paine was deeply influenced by his father's Quaker values. His abiding commitment to social equality and justice and his outspoken condemnation of the degradation and destructiveness of war were rooted in those early lessons at the Quaker meetinghouse. "If there is a sin superior to every other," Paine would write years later, "it is that of willful and offensive war."

Typically, a boy of the lower classes began working in his father's shop at an early age. Not only was the extra hand essential in the shop, but without the knowledge of a skilled trade, a young man would be doomed to a life of unemployment and poverty. Paine's father, however, saved enough money to provide his son with an education. From age 6 to age 13, Thomas attended the Thetford Grammar School. He learned to read and write and showed a natural talent for the sciences. His instructor, who had traveled widely as a young man, stirred the young boy's imagination by telling tales of his adventures at sea and long voyages to far-off places. Intrigued by these stories, Thomas read every book

The history . . . is that of an English mechanic, of Quaker training, caught in political cyclones of the last century, and set at the center of its revolutions, in the old world and the new.

—MONCURE D. CONWAY
American historian, on
Paine's life

about America that he could find in the school's tiny library. After reading *A Natural History of Virginia*, a vivid narrative of the conquering of the New World, Paine said, "My inclination from that day for seeing the western side of the Atlantic never left me."

Paine was not a brilliant student. He never mastered Latin, which in the 18th century was indispensable for a professional career in medicine or law. One contemporary wrote that he was a "sharp boy of unsettled application" who "left no performances which denote a juvenile vigor of uncommon attainments." At age 13, Paine's parents removed

The English scientist Isaac Newton experiments with light in his study. Newton, who first propounded the idea of universal gravity, believed in the existence of natural laws that could be understood by human reason. Paine was greatly influenced by Newton's work.

The English warship *the Terrible*. Filled with wanderlust, 16-year-old Thomas Paine boarded the ship in hopes of pursuing a career as a sailor. Though his father, who was aware of the hardships of a seafaring life, promptly retrieved him, the determined young man soon signed aboard a private vessel, the *King of Prussia*.

him from the school and put him to work as an apprentice staymaker in his father's shop. His father was a skilled artisan, and under his tutelage Paine became an accomplished craftsman in his own right. The manual dexterity and practical skills he developed would be invaluable to his later work as an amateur scientist and inventor.

Yet wanderlust and the desire to achieve greater success must have burned deep in the boy's heart. At age 16, Paine ran away from home to seek his fortune as a sailor on a warship, aptly named *The Terrible*. Paine's father followed the young runaway and persuaded him to return home. Not long after he was rescued, however, Paine left again and signed aboard another privateer, the *King of Prussia*. Paine never reminisced about his days as a sailor, but shipboard life for a young man must have been arduous. Conditions at sea were brutal: Disease and sickness were endemic and discipline was strictly enforced.

In 1757, at age 20, Paine landed in London as a journeyman staymaker. A year later, he moved to Dover on the southeastern coast. The following year, his master loaned Paine enough money to set up his own shop in the town of Sandwich. In September 1759, Paine married Mary Lambert, a maid employed by the wife of a local shopkeeper. Paine's shop did not prosper, and a few months after his marriage he and his wife moved to Margate to escape his debts. A year later, Paine's wife died; although some historians have maintained that she died during a premature childbirth, the circumstances of her death are shrouded in mystery. In all his many works, Paine never wrote about his first wife, nor did he speak about her to his friends.

At age 24, Paine temporarily abandoned staymaking and returned to his parents' home in Thetford to study for the qualifying examination for a position in the excise service. The excise service was a government agency that collected customs taxes imposed on common consumption items, such as tea. After a year's preparation, Paine passed the exam and in 1764 received his first posting in the town of Alford.

Paine's job was to ride his horse along the North Sea coast on the lookout for smugglers bringing in contraband. An exciseman's position was dangerous and unpopular; indeed, due to the heavy taxes, public sympathy was with the smugglers. Because the excisemen's salaries were so meager, corruption was widespread in the service; many inspectors approved their consignments without carefully examining, or even looking at, the contents. In July 1765, a year after receiving his post, Paine was dismissed from the service for just this offense. For the next two years Paine barely eked out a living working as a staymaker and teacher. In July 1767, Paine applied for readmission to the excise service and was promised a new post the following year.

In 1768, Paine was appointed to a position in Lewes, where he would live for the next six years. Now 31 years of age, he was 5 feet 9 inches tall, a slender man with a large nose and bright blue eyes. Paine lived with the family of Samuel Ollive, a Quaker who owned a small tobacco shop and was involved in the town's political affairs. After Ollive died, Paine helped his widow and his daughter Elizabeth with the running of the shop. In March 1771, he married Elizabeth, 10 years his junior.

Thoughts are a kind of mental smoke which require words to illuminate them.
—THOMAS PAINE
excerpt from a letter to Benjamin Franklin

Paine was popular among the townspeople, and he had many friends and acquaintances. The center of Paine's life was the men's social club that met evenings at the White Hart Tavern for lively political discussions. Paine was widely recognized for his skillful debating. Eloquent, witty, even obstinate in his opinions, Paine reveled in the furious give-and-take of political conversation. His notoriety was such that a candidate for Parliament asked him to write an election song for his campaign.

In 1772, the excise officers throughout England decided to lobby Parliament for a salary increase. Paine was urged to write a pamphlet on their behalf by his friend George Scott, a member of the excise

Two bound excise officers are taunted and humiliated by smugglers wielding whips. Because their job was to collect taxes, excise officers were extremely unpopular. Paine held an excise officer's post for several years.

board, who was friends with such luminaries as Edward Gibbon, Samuel Johnson, and Benjamin Franklin. Paine's pamphlet was a forceful, clear, well-reasoned piece of writing; in what became the hallmark of his works, the prose was simple and could be read by any literate person in the street. Paine argued that it made no sense, indeed was counterproductive, to underpay inspectors for a service that was so prone to corruption. Paine insisted that higher pay for the officers would ultimately generate more revenue for the government.

Paine's essay also implicitly maintained that government officials who had never experienced poverty firsthand could never truly comprehend the allurement that corruption held for the impoverished excise officers. Although Paine's appeal was ultimately unsuccessful, he had embarked on what would be a long career as a political pamphleteer. In the late 18th century, with increasing numbers of middle-class people learning to read and printers

Alehouse patrons take part in a rousing political discussion. Paine, who loved to debate political issues, frequented a pub called the White Hart Tavern, where he could usually engage an enthusiastic adversary over a pint of ale.

Benjamin Franklin, successful publisher and renowned statesman, was impressed with Paine's abilities as a writer and political theorist. He introduced the young pamphleteer to many of London's scientific luminaries and wrote a letter of recommendation, which Paine carried with him to America in 1774.

and booksellers flourishing in every city, political propagandists, such as Paine, would achieve widespread influence and prestige through the power of the printed word.

Paine moved to London in 1772 to lobby full time for the excisemen's cause. Paine's stay in London exposed him to the broader currents of British political radicalism, which proclaimed the importance of individual liberty and the right to resist tyrannical and unjust governments; his political philosophy was deeply influenced by these radical themes.

In London, Paine was introduced to Benjamin Franklin, who at the time was serving as the commercial agent for the American colonies. The quintessential self-made man, Franklin was a prosperous businessman and a distinguished political leader. He was equally well known for his numerous scientific experiments and inventions. Although 30 years Paine's senior, Franklin felt a strong affinity for the young pamphleteer, who shared the older man's passion for both science and politics. Through Franklin, Paine met a number of renowned mathematicians, astronomers, and scientists. He attended lectures regularly and even purchased equipment to conduct his own scientific experiments.

Compared with the heady atmosphere of London, Paine's life in Lewes must have seemed dull. After spending so much time in the capital, he had little time to devote to his small grocery shop or to his excise career. As a result, the shop went bankrupt and Paine was dismissed from the excise service in 1774.

Then, matters got worse for Paine. In June 1774, he and his wife agreed to a separation. Considering their breakup an entirely personal matter, Paine never confided to his friends the reason his marriage had failed. "I had cause for it, but I will name it to no one," he said. Thereafter, Paine would have many close friendships with women, but he would never remarry.

With his marriage and career in ruins, Paine told Franklin that he would seek a fresh start in America. He obtained a letter of introduction from Franklin: "The bearer Mr. Thomas Paine is very well recommended to me as an ingenious young man." With the money he received from his separation settlement, Paine bought a first-class ticket on the *London Packet* and sailed for the New World in September 1774. After 37 years of disappointments and frustrated dreams, this would be Paine's last chance to make something of his life.

The discharged and insulted postmaster could sympathize with the dismissed and starving exciseman. Franklin . . . believed [Paine] would be useful and successful in America.
—MONCURE D. CONWAY
American historian

COMMON SENSE;

ADDRESSED TO THE

INHABITANTS

OF

AMERICA,

On the following interesting

SUBJECTS.

I. Of the Origin and Design of Government in general, with concise Remarks on the English Constitution.

II. Of Monarchy and Hereditary Succession.

III. Thoughts on the present State of American Affairs.

IV. Of the present Ability of America, with some miscellaneous Reflections.

Man knows no Master save creating HEAVEN,
Or those whom choice and common good ordain.

THOMSON.

PHILADELPHIA;

Printed, and Sold, by R. BELL, in Third-Street.

MDCCLXXVI.

2

A Special Genius

Paine's passage to America was a harrowing journey, mainly because of a typhus epidemic on board ship. When Paine arrived in Philadelphia on November 30, 1774, he was in a weakened, feverish condition and had to be carried on a stretcher. With so many afflicted with the disease, doctors worked furiously to attend to all those who needed treatment, and some had to wait while others received care. However, when it was learned that Paine was carrying letters of recommendation from Franklin, he was promptly placed in the hospital and given special attention. In fact, once he recovered, Paine found that Franklin's introduction opened many doors. He quickly found work tutoring the sons of some of Philadelphia's wealthiest citizens.

Paine arrived in America at a time when tension between the colonies and England was mounting. Since the early 1700s, the colonies had developed an independent political and economic identity that now threatened to disrupt England's colonial poli-

Your countenancing me has obtained for me many friends and much reputation, for which please accept my sincere thanks.
—THOMAS PAINE
excerpt from a letter to
Benjamin Franklin

In 1776, Paine, living in Philadelphia, penned a political pamphlet called *Common Sense*, in which he criticized England's colonial policies and urged America to fight for its independence. The pamphlet marked an early episode in Paine's lifelong campaign for republicanism and American self-determination.

The English general George Washington (center) raises his hat as the British flag is hoisted at Fort Duquesne, Pennsylvania, during the French and Indian War. England secured its control over North America by emerging victorious in this war, but it was left with a huge war debt and looming financial commitments in its newly acquired territories.

cies. Whereas England assumed that its sovereign authority extended to the colonies by way of the royal governors, the American colonists considered their own elected legislature to be preeminent with respect to domestic issues.

The tension had an economic basis as well as a political one. Ever since the passage of the Navigation Acts of 1673 and 1696 by the English Parliament, the American colonies were locked into an inequitable trade relationship with England. The colonists were unable to trade directly with other European nations: Their exports—primarily cotton, tobacco, and sugar — had to be shipped first to England, where middlemen would then sell the goods for a profit on the European market. Similarly,

America could only purchase European products through English merchants, at prices far higher than if the goods had been bought on the open market. Although loose enforcement of the regulations often made illicit trade possible, the arrangement nevertheless constituted a serious economic burden on the American colonies.

The turning point in colonial relations came after England's victory over France in 1763 in the French and Indian War. Though the victory gave England decisive control over the North American continent, it left England with a huge national debt and the daunting financial prospect of maintaining a large standing army in America in order to administer its new territorial acquisitions. Therefore, England attempted to tighten the administration and enforcement of colonial regulations and to compel the colonies to bear their cost of the empire.

New legislation — the Stamp Act of 1765 and the Tea Act of 1773 — was implemented in order to generate increased revenue for the Crown, but each measure provoked fierce protest throughout the colonies. In the most memorable protest on December

The Boston Tea Party. England tried to force the colonies to bear the burden of maintaining the British Empire by imposing heavy taxes on imports and requiring the colonies to trade exclusively with England. One of the most celebrated demonstrations to protest these measures was this one in Boston harbor.

Patrick Henry addresses the First Continental Congress, at Carpenter's Hall, Philadelphia, in 1774. Following the Boston Tea Party, the British closed Boston harbor and established a military presence there to inhibit further demonstrations. Delegates to the congress met to discuss possible countermeasures.

16, 1773, a group of colonists masquerading as Indians boarded three English ships in Boston harbor and dumped their cargo, mainly tea, into the water. In response to the Boston Tea Party, the British closed Boston harbor and sent General Thomas Gage to Massachusetts as a military governor, with orders to crack down on colonial protests. Many colonial leaders feared that these measures would be extended to the other colonies, and they organized a meeting to discuss appropriate countermeasures. On September 5, 1774, the First Continental Congress was convened, with delegates from all the colonies except Georgia. The Continental Congress demanded the repeal of all objectionable laws passed since 1763. They issued a proclamation asserting the colonies' inalienable rights, and they established a new continental association to enforce a boycott of British goods should their demands not be met. Even though national independence was not yet on the agenda, the delegates, led by militant colonists Samuel Adams and Richard Henry Lee, rejected a proposal for reconciliation with England.

Robert Aitken, a Scottish immigrant printer, began a new publishing venture, the *Pennsylvania Magazine*, in January 1775, and he persuaded Paine to join him. Paine wrote the introduction to the first issue and henceforth handled the daily operations of the magazine. Under Paine's tutelage, the magazine's circulation climbed from 600 to 1,500, making it the most popular periodical in America. In the first months, Paine was uncharacteristically reticent to write about American political affairs; he devoted most of his efforts to poetry or literary articles. One of Paine's poems, "On the Death of General Wolfe," a memorial to the heroic British general who had defeated the French in Canada, received great acclaim.

Paine's first substantive comment on the unsettled American political scene was an impassioned article in March 1775, attacking slavery. Paine argued that the institution of slavery violated the inherent right to freedom of every individual. Slavery was "contrary to the right of nature, to every principle of justice and humanity." He condemned the proponents of slavery for using select quotations from the Bible to justify "this wicked practice." Paine particularly denounced the hypocrisy of the southern colonists who protested their unjust treatment at the hands of the British yet perpetuated such a pernicious practice as slavery. He urged Americans to "discontinue and renounce the practice of slavery" and suggested that land in the fron-

Paine took a position as an editor and writer for the *Pennsylvania Magazine* in 1775. At first he wrote mainly literary pieces; later he wrote thoughtful, impassioned essays on the pressing political issues of the day.

A plantation owner supervises his slaves. In March 1775, Paine wrote an antislavery tract for *Pennsylvania Magazine*, in which he urged Americans to free their slaves. Though others had criticized the institution of slavery, few had argued against it as eloquently as Paine did.

tier territories be set aside for the settlement of liberated blacks. Paine's was not the first voice to be raised against slavery, but he provided a compelling argument for the abolitionists' cause. A month after his article was published, the first antislavery movement, the American Antislavery Society, was founded in Philadelphia.

By the spring of 1775, colonial politics had become increasingly volatile. King George decided a show of military force was necessary to assert British sovereignty against the upstart Americans. On April 19, 1775, a detachment of 1,200 British soldiers left Boston to destroy the military supplies Massachusetts colonists had gathered at Concord. Alerted by Paul Revere, the colonial minutemen surprised the British soldiers at Lexington; when the smoke cleared from the famous "shots heard round the world," 8 Americans lay dead, with another 10 wounded. The English troops marched to Concord and destroyed the supply depot, but they returned to Boston under a hail of musket fire from thousands of enraged colonists. British forces suffered 273 dead and wounded in this first battle of the American Revolution.

Although other battles soon followed, the war mood subsided by late summer, and sympathy for a policy of reconciliation with England was widespread. The primary focus of the Second Continental Congress, which began in May 1775, was the debate between advocates of independence and friends of reconciliation. Although the delegates prudently selected George Washington to be commander in chief of the American army and made plans to place the colonies in a state of defense, there were, nevertheless, powerful voices raised against independence. Many delegates did not believe America's meager forces stood a chance of defeating the most powerful nation in the world.

Perhaps more than anyone, Thomas Paine provided the spark for independence. Although "no one had been a warmer wisher for reconciliation" than Paine before April 19, 1775, the Battle of Lexington decisively ended Paine's fence-sitting. Henceforth, Paine was an outspoken proponent of American in-

Paul Revere warns citizens of the coming of the "redcoats" on the evening of April 18, 1775. The following day, the British clashed with the colonial militia in Massachusetts at Lexington and Concord, beginning the American Revolution.

dependence, and in October he became one of the first to state publicly that a break from England was inevitable. In November, Paine was urged by his friend Benjamin Rush to write a pamphlet that would present the case for independence. Paine began writing on November 1, 1775, just as news arrived that King George had refused to accept the Continental Congress's peace petition and had declared the American colonies to be in rebellion. Paine's essay, *Common Sense*, was published in January 1776. A brilliant argument for independence and for the superiority of republican government over hereditary monarchy, the pamphlet transformed the terms of political debate in America and made Paine an internationally known figure.

Common Sense began with a devastating critique of hereditary monarchy. Most Americans believed that the British constitutional monarchy, a complex system of checks and balances between the king and legislature, was the ideal system of government. Paine utterly destroyed this image once and for all. The divine right of kings to rule, he insisted, was a

Confrontation on Concord Bridge. In the battles of Lexington and Concord, the American minutemen suffered 10 casualties and the destruction of a supply depot; 273 British soldiers were killed or wounded.

George Washington was named commander in chief of the American army by the Second Continental Congress in June 1775. Though he accepted the appointment, he did so reluctantly because he was not to be paid for his service.

mockery. The moral and intellectual characteristics needed to govern were not something that could be inherited; indeed, under monarchical systems, more often than not, power fell into the hands of incompetent fools, such as King George. Paine argued that hereditary rule was inherently unjust: "No generation has the right to impose its choices upon posterity; whatever government or form of society was right for one generation might be totally unsuited to the differing needs of another."

Paine's denunciation of the monarchy was brutally frank: He called King George the "royal brute of England" and stated "of more worth is one honest man to society and in the sight of God than all the crowned ruffians that ever lived." For Paine, the overriding issue was the need for a republican government; no system of checks and balances would be possible so long as the monarchy existed. "The nearer any government approaches to a republic," he said, "the less need there is for a King." Years before his contemporaries suggested similar ideas, Paine called for the establishment of a republican government in America, with a written constitution that guaranteed civil liberties, broad franchise and regular elections, and a national legislature.

Paine then discussed the state of British-American relations. Offering "nothing more than simple facts, plain arguments, and common sense," Paine asserted that formal ties to England would constantly embroil America in distant European disputes, would hinder the colonies' economic growth, and would stunt the development of democracy. Paine envisaged a neutral, independent America, one that would pursue a policy of friendship and free trade with every country. Independence was inevitable; those who speak of reconciliation are "weak men who cannot see, prejudiced men who will not see." Paine concluded his essay with an inspiring vision of the true meaning of American independence. "We have it in our power to begin the world over again," he proclaimed, "the birthday of a new world is at hand."

Paine's special genius was his gift for rendering complex political issues perfectly understandable to the average citizen. A true child of the Enlightenment, Paine sincerely believed that every person had the ability to understand complicated political questions. Accordingly, his rhetoric was designed to reach the widest audience possible. He wrote, "As it is my design to make those that can scarcely read understand, I shall therefore avoid every literary ornament and put it in language as plain as the alphabet." Paine used vocabulary, metaphors, and images that were derived from the common experiences of citizens. He did not mask his sense of outrage nor couch his arguments in the measured language of most of his contemporaries.

The success of *Common Sense* was astounding. At a time when an average pamphlet sold only a few thousand copies, *Common Sense* sold 150,000. The pamphlet struck a resonant chord in the colonies, winning many new converts to the cause of independence. George Washington said it worked "a powerful change in the minds of many men." A Connecticut man stated, "We were blind, but on reading these enlightening words the scales have fallen from our eyes."

King George III of England. Though he did not possess absolute power under the British system, George III was the primary force behind the policies that led to war with the colonies. Paine frequently ridiculed the British monarch in his writing.

3

Spirit and Ingenuity

Within weeks of the publication of *Common Sense*, sentiment for independence rose dramatically, and during the next six months a torrent of articles, letters, and pamphlets were written in support of Paine's positions. On July 2, 1776, the Continental Congress declared the colonies free and independent states, and two days later they approved the Declaration of Independence, written by Thomas Jefferson.

In the meantime, Great Britain's military forces were advancing on the colonies. That July, a fleet of more than 250 ships landed 30,000 British troops — the largest expeditionary force ever mounted by England — on the shores of Staten Island, New York. The British troops were seasoned professionals led by the experienced General William Howe, whereas George Washington, commander in chief of the American forces, had only 10,000 troops at his command, the majority of whom were ill equipped and largely untrained. Americans feared that Washington's motley crew would be no match for Howe's elite brigades.

Common Sense burst from the press with an effect which has rarely been produced by types and paper in any age or country.
—BENJAMIN RUSH
American patriot

Benjamin Franklin, John Adams, and Thomas Jefferson (left to right), delegates to the Continental Congress, collaborate on the writing of the Declaration of Independence in 1776. Jefferson was selected to be the principal author of the declaration because he was from the largest colony, Virginia, had few enemies, and was a superb writer.

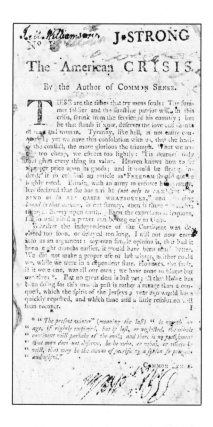

The opening page of Paine's first pamphlet, *Crisis*. Paine published 16 such periodicals on the American struggle for independence, and in each one he argued vehemently against both monarchy and foreign domination. The essays inspired American soldiers and citizens alike.

Still, Paine predicted that the British army would be unable to conquer the colonies. He wrote, "In all the wars which you have formerly been concerned in you only had armies to contend with; in this case, you have both an army and a country to combat." Paine believed that in the American colonists England faced an opponent whose will to win was greater than their own.

On the battlefield, the truth seemed to the contrary. After several disastrous battles in New York, Washington led his beleaguered troops on a retreat across New Jersey. The winter weather had arrived, and while the British were encamped in plush, warm quarters in Trenton, Washington's ragged men camped out in the cold along the western bank of the Delaware River. Morale in the army reached a new low. In early December, Paine began writing the first of 16 pamphlets entitled *The Crisis*, which he hoped would stir the "passion of patriotism." Its opening lines read as follows:

> These are the times that try men's souls. The summer soldier and the sunshine patriot will, in this crisis, shrink from the service of their country; but he that stands it *now* deserves the love and thanks of man and woman. Tyranny, like hell, is not easily conquered; yet we have this consolation with us, that the harder the conflict, the more glorious the triumph."

Once again, Paine's words turned the tide of events. The pamphlet was printed on December 19, and within days copies were being read and passed around by the weary soldiers at Washington's headquarters. Paine's inspiration gave the Americans a new resolve and lifted the mood of defeatism.

With renewed spirit among his troops, Washington planned a surprise attack to reverse America's fortunes. On Christmas night, December 25, 1776, Washington's army boarded a flotilla of wooden boats and began a perilous journey across the icy Delaware River. Upon disembarking, the minutemen, carrying over 150 pieces of artillery, silently marched in the pitch-black night toward Trenton. Chilled to the bone and blinded by the falling snow, the American army traveled the nine miles to Trenton in less than four hours. At dawn, the Americans attacked the sleeping British and Hessian forces, capturing hundreds.

The next decisive military confrontation took place in Saratoga, New York, in 1778. There, on October 17, the British general John Burgoyne was forced to surrender his army to Horatio Gates. When news of the American victory reached Paris in early December, the French government decided to join the war openly on the side of the Americans. Members of Congress learned of the French alliance in April 1779, just in time to nullify the efforts of a British peace commission. The French support dramatically altered the course of the war; henceforth, the combination of French naval power and American ground forces would tilt the balance of power to the American side. The alliance also provided the backdrop to one of the greatest controversies of Paine's career.

Washington and his men cross the icy Delaware River on December 25, 1776. The next morning, the American militia surprised the sleeping British and Hessian troops in Trenton, achieving one of the most decisive victories of the revolutionary war.

In early 1777, Paine accepted a clerical position with the Committee of Foreign Affairs. The most important area of foreign relations for the United States at that time was undoubtedly the diplomatic initiative with France. Before the two countries formed a formal alliance, France had agreed to support America in its struggle for independence by providing financial aid and supplies. In 1776, a commission led by Arthur Lee and Silas Deane was sent to Paris to procure supplies. The French were eager to assist the American revolutionaries but, wanting to maintain the appearance of neutrality, they insisted the aid be kept a secret. A dummy firm was created, under the command of Caron de Beaumarchais, so that the arms could seemingly be sent under the guise of normal export trade, without any

British general John Burgoyne surrenders to Horatio Gates in Saratoga, New York, on November 17, 1777. Following the American victory at Saratoga, the French joined the war on the side of the colonists, greatly shifting the balance of power against the British.

hint of involvement by the French crown. Deane, as commercial agent, was to be paid a five percent commission for all supplies purchased.

The heated controversy that developed centered around whether the supplies that the Americans received were actually a gift from the French government — which would invalidate Deane's commission — or whether they had been legitimately purchased. Beaumarchais, who had a reputation for shady dealings, sold gunpowder, uniforms, and swords for profit; some weapons that had been donated by the French army were sold at half their original cost. Although Lee informed Deane that most of the matériel was a French gift, Deane insisted on claiming a commission on all the transactions. Deane's return to America in the summer of 1778 caused a political scandal; many members of Congress knew Deane had used the transaction to line his own pockets.

The Deane affair involved much more substantial issues than the impropriety of a single man. Earlier in 1778, Congress had been shocked by revelations that corrupt government officials were profiting from their public service. War profiteering had become a remarkably lucrative venture, creating personal fortunes for many unethical American merchants who used their government positions to gain personal wealth.

The staunchest opponents of profiteering were Richard Lee, Henry Laurens, and Samuel Adams, who were among Paine's closest associates. They took the lead in condemning Deane's actions, but their calls for an independent investigation were stymied by Deane's powerful supporters. Lee and Laurens were viciously smeared in the press, and Laurens was forced to resign as president of Congress under a storm of criticism. Paine, who had refrained from entering the controversy, felt obliged to speak out now that his friends' reputations were at stake.

In his *Letter to Silas Deane*, published in December 1778, Paine inferred that the French arms were a gift to America and hence that Deane was a scoundrel. Paine had learned of Deane's duplicity by virtue

The American lawyer and diplomat Silas Deane was sent to Paris to procure war supplies from the French government. His shady dealings led to charges of embezzlement, which Paine, in his *Letter to Silas Deane*, helped to substantiate.

The American statesman Henry Laurens. Elected president of the Continental Congress in 1777, Laurens, who had called for an independent investigation of Deane, resigned a year later under pressure from Deane's supporters, many of whom were powerful figures in government and the press.

of his position as secretary of the Committee of Foreign Affairs, which made him privy to the secret diplomatic correspondence between France and America. By revealing classified information, however, Paine broke his pledge to remain silent about the committee's affairs. Because this indiscretion embarrassed the French government, which had been trying to maintain the guise of neutrality, the French ambassador promptly called for Paine's resignation from the committee.

Paine resigned his post on January 8, 1779. Shortly afterward France offered him $1,000 a year to write pro-French propaganda, but Paine indignantly refused this thinly veiled bribe. In the months after his resignation, Paine wrote numerous essays denouncing Deane and attacking his congressional critics.

In the aftermath of the Deane affair, Paine's role as the leading propagandist for the American Revolution temporarily subsided. While Washington's army spent its second bitter winter at Valley Forge, Paine worked in Philadelphia as a clerk for his friend Owen Biddle. He did not write another *Crisis* pamphlet for almost 18 months. Instead, he threw himself into Pennsylvania politics — serving on state legislative committees, writing reports, and meeting often with his friends and colleagues to discuss legislative proposals.

After a few desultory campaigns in 1779, the British regained the offensive in 1780, this time in the South, where they took advantage of the strong Loyalist sentiment of much of the local population. By April, the British completely controlled Georgia, and on May 12, 1780, the city of Charleston surrendered.

The British victories were clear evidence that the American war effort needed to be revitalized. New supplies and funds were desperately needed, but this looked to be impossible. Though each state was supposed to raise its own funds for the war effort, many state legislatures did not levy sufficient taxes to meet prescribed quotas. Determined to do his part, Paine donated $500 and created an emergency fund to supply Washington's depleted army. He hoped his generosity would spur the more affluent to follow his lead. "I feel the utmost concern that the fairest cause that men ever engaged in, and with the fairest prospect of success," he wrote, "should now be sunk so low, and that not from any new ability in the enemy, but from a willful neglect and decay of every species of public spirit in ourselves."

Paine traveled to France in February 1781 to petition the French government for additional credit and supplies. Upon his return to the United States in August, Paine witnessed the commencement of the decisive confrontation of the war at Yorktown. In early 1781, a new American offensive drove the British army out of Georgia and the Carolinas. General Charles Cornwallis and his army retreated to Yorktown, Virginia, where they entrenched behind massive fortifications. The British sent a fleet of 19 ships to rescue Cornwallis's troops, but they were repulsed by Admiral de Grasse's French fleet of 28 ships.

Washington and his troops try to shelter themselves against the bitter cold wind at Valley Forge. The men were so poorly supplied that many of them were without boots or a blanket. Some wrapped their feet in rags while others walked barefoot on the snow and ice.

When Washington realized that the French victory had virtually eliminated all hopes of a British escape by sea, he readied his forces from New York to Virginia. In September, his army linked up with the French troops under the command of the marquis de Lafayette and surrounded the British forces at Yorktown in Virginia. On October 19, 1781, Cornwallis surrendered his force of 8,000. There would be a few minor skirmishes during the next year, but the colonies had effectively won their independence at Yorktown. On April 17, 1783, Congress proclaimed an end to the war.

"The times that tryed [sic] men's souls are over — and the greatest and completest revolution that the world ever knew, gloriously and happily accomplished," wrote Paine in the *Crisis* published on

On October 17, 1781, Washington's troops defeated those of British general Charles Cornwallis, effectively ending the American revolutionary war. Two days later the surrender of the British general's sword served as a ceremonious end to the six-year struggle for independence.

April 19, 1783, the eighth anniversary of the battles of Lexington and Concord. The American Revolution, he proclaimed, "has contributed more to enlighten the world and diffuse a spirit of freedom and liberality among mankind than any other human event . . . that ever preceded it." Paine had played a vital role in the American success. As John Adams astutely commented, "Washington's sword would have been wielded in vain had it not been supported by the pen of Paine." The American Revolution, which had "made the world happy," had transformed an anonymous refugee into one of the most celebrated citizens of the world.

For all his fame and prestige, Paine enjoyed little in the way of material fortune from his eight-year stay in America. In the years after the war, Paine had no real means of support and often lived in near destitution. After the American victory at Yorktown, Paine wrote a long letter to Washington complaining of his impoverished condition. "While it was everybody's fate to suffer," he said, "I cheerfully suffered with them." But now that the financial crisis had passed and the country was moving into prosperity, he thought it only fair that something should be done on his behalf. Washington spoke with Robert Morris on several occasions to urge him to find some sort of employment for Paine. Morris met Paine in early 1782 and told him that the country needed the valuable services of its most respected writer. Although the war was over, there were still a great number of issues yet to be resolved, and Paine's special talents would be invaluable in helping to develop clearheaded policies.

In February, Paine agreed to accept a salary of $800 to serve as propagandist for the American government. During the next 18 months, Paine wrote numerous essays, including a fierce denunciation of England's attempt to bribe France out of its alliance with America.

Once the peace treaty with Great Britain was signed, Paine's assignment was terminated, and his sad financial situation intensified. His revolutionary writings had been widely circulated, but Paine

> *What I write is pure nature, and my pen and my soul have ever gone together. My writings I have always given away, receiving only the expense of printing and paper, and sometimes not even that.*
> —THOMAS PAINE
> responding to rumors that he profited from his publications

had not profited from their sale. In fact, he had used his own funds to ensure their distribution, and he had donated the proceeds of several editions to the war effort. He had used what little money he possessed to buy a small home in Bordentown, New Jersey. His reputation was better than ever — people greeted him on the streets and toasted him in taverns — but he desired a more tangible reward for his services to the Revolution.

Paine decided to appeal directly to Congress. He knew that many members of Congress would be reluctant to grant him any reward for his wartime writing when so many of the men who had actually served in the Continental Army still remained unpaid, but he pointed out that these men, "had estates and fortunes to defend and . . . now have them to enjoy." He went on, "But with me it is otherwise. I had no other inducement than principle, and have nothing else to enjoy." Congress offered Paine a paid position as official historian of the Revolution, but Paine declined, insisting he be compensated for his past services.

In June 1784, New York gave Paine a 267-acre farm in New Rochelle, which had been confiscated from a Tory Loyalist. The declaration that accompanied the bequest stated that Paine's works had "inspired the citizens of this state with unanimity, confirmed their confidence in the rectitude of their cause, and have ultimately contributed to the freedom, sovereignty, and independence of the United States." New Rochelle hosted a ceremony for Paine, and almost the entire village was in attendance. He personally greeted and shook hands with everyone in the crowd and even helped stir sugar into the whiskey punch that had been prepared for the celebratory toasts. Paine did not keep his permanent residence in New Rochelle; most of his close friends lived in Philadelphia or New Jersey, and the house was much too large in any case for just one man living alone.

Both Washington and Jefferson remained Paine's strongest supporters and worked behind the scenes to secure him further funding. Washington wrote personal entreaties to members of the Virginia Assembly. "Can nothing be done in our Assembly for

> *This is a government that has nothing to fear. It needs no proclamation to deter people from reading and writing. . . . It was by encouraging discussion and rendering the press free upon all subjects of government that the principles of government became understood in America.*
>
> —THOMAS PAINE
> on the new continental government of America

poor Paine?" he wrote. "Must the merits and services of *Common Sense* continue to slide down the streams of time, unrewarded by this country? His writings have certainly had a powerful effect upon the public mind — ought they not then to meet an adequate return?" The Virginia legislature voted in favor of a bill providing a land grant to Paine, but it was never finalized. The Pennsylvania Assembly awarded him $500, and on October 6, 1785, Congress finally voted him an award of $3,000.

With his financial burdens eased, Paine was able to return to the enjoyment of a quiet life and his scientific interests. Paine was close friends with the luminaries of the Philadelphia scientific community — David Rittenhouse, William Henry, and his old friend Benjamin Franklin. Paine shared both their

The American politician and businessman Robert Morris served as superintendent of finance under the Articles of Confederation and was a delegate to the Continental Congress. He used his skills in money matters to help finance the American war for independence.

love of experimentation and their devotion to practical ingenuity.

Perhaps Paine's most inspired creation was his design for an iron bridge. The idea for the bridge came one winter day during one of Paine's customary afternoon walks, when he noticed the gigantic ice floe in the Schuylkill River. At the time, the only way to cross the river was by ferry, which in winter was often out of service because of the dangerous ice. Conventional bridge design, typically a wooden bridge resting atop stone piers laid in the riverbed, would be ineffective for the Schuylkill because the heavy ice might dislodge the unstable piers. Paine conceived of a bridge composed of a single arch — with 13 ribs to commemorate the 13 United States — that could span the river without piers. The bridge's iron girders, arranged crisscross as in a spider's web, would evenly distribute the weight to

The astronomer David Rittenhouse, a close friend of Paine's, held several important posts in the Pennsylvania state government, including assemblyman during the revolutionary war and, later, state treasurer. In 1792 he was named the first director of the U.S. Mint.

the piers at each end of the bridge. Paine did not invent the iron bridge; a single-arch bridge had been erected in England in 1779. Nevertheless, his bridge featured an innovative design and a length of more than 400 feet, which was unprecedented.

Paine converted some rooms in his house into a workshop and hired a young carpenter to assist him in constructing a model bridge. Once the wooden model was completed, Paine began casting one in wrought iron. When the iron model was finished, in December 1786, Paine shipped it to Benjamin Franklin's house in Philadelphia. There, he convinced Franklin, Rittenhouse, and another friend to walk across the top of the model, which easily withstood the weight of the three men.

On New Year's Day, the model was exhibited at the Pennsylvania State Assembly. Despite their firsthand view, members of the State Assembly rejected Paine's proposal to construct his bridge over the Schuylkill. A number of prominent architects and engineers testified that his design was sound, but the legislators remained somewhat skeptical that Paine, known primarily for his literary accomplishments, could actually build a safe bridge. Paine's proposal was also expensive; the estimated construction cost was more than $300,000, more than the state's entire annual budget. The state was unwilling to commit sufficient financing, nor was Paine able to attract any private investors to risk funds for such a speculative venture.

Franklin told Paine that one possible way to win approval from the assembly would be to obtain an endorsement for his design from the two most prestigious scientific societies in Europe; namely, the Royal Society in London and the Royal Academy of Sciences in Paris. The idea of returning to Europe appealed to Paine, so he packed his model and belongings. Franklin wrote letters of recommendation to his influential friends in Paris and London and urged Thomas Jefferson, now U.S. ambassador to France, to introduce Paine to the appropriate people. On April 26, 1787, Paine sailed for Europe. He planned only a brief trip, but it would be another 15 years before he returned to America.

> *The mere independence of America, were it to have been followed by a system of government modelled after the corrupt system of the English government, would not have interested me with the unabated ardor that it did.*
> —THOMAS PAINE

4

"Living to Some Purpose"

After a four-day journey through the beautiful French countryside, Paine reached Paris on May 26, 1787. In Paris, he was welcomed by Jean-Baptiste Le Roy, a prominent member of the Academy of Sciences and the director of the prestigious King's Laboratory at Passy. Le Roy, a close friend of Franklin's, graciously introduced Paine to important members of the academy who would be instrumental in approving his bridge project. The city of Paris had solicited proposals for a new bridge over the Seine, so Paine, confident that his bridge would be ideal in terms of both style and cost, sent the model to the academy. A committee that included several celebrated mathematicians was promptly established to review Paine's proposal.

While the committee deliberated, Paine became acquainted with the salon society of the French elite. Jefferson introduced him to the marquis de Lafayette, the young nobleman who had defied his family by joining the American army in the War of Independence. Lafayette's circle of friends included

The novelty or discovery in Paine's bridge was in the arrangement of the segments of the arch on the principle of a spider's web.
—ALFRED O. ALDRIDGE
Paine biographer

A 1789 French cartoon characterizes the plight of the French people. The masses are depicted as bound, gagged, blindfolded, and bleeding while straining under the weight of their oppressors — the nobility, the clergy, and the monarchical bureaucracy.

Members of the French aristocracy attend a ball at the Palace of Versailles. When Paine arrived in France in 1787, Jean-Baptiste Le Roy, a friend of Benjamin Franklin's, introduced the young political writer to some of French society's most celebrated figures.

many of France's most prominent political leaders and scientists, such as the duc de Rochefoucauld and the marquis de Condorcet, the illustrious mathematician and philosopher. It was a splendid time for Paine, as he exchanged opinions and shared confidences with the cream of French society. He seemed totally unaware of the political ferment beneath the cosmopolitan surface of French politics.

For more than two centuries, the French monarch ruled by divine right and possessed absolute authority over France's state bureaucracy, which pervaded all of French society, while the French aristocracy enjoyed an ostentatious court life and a privileged relationship with the state. Aristocrats received appointments within the bureaucracy and paid no taxes. The clergy was similarly exempt from taxation, as was the bourgeoisie. Because so much of France's wealth went untaxed, the monarch increased the tax burden on the poor peasantry, who made up the vast majority of the population. Before long, the angry, overtaxed masses were on the verge of rebellion.

France's involvement in the American War of Independence put a great strain on the state's finances. In order to meet France's financial obligations at home and abroad, King Louis XVI asked the nobility and clergy to consider certain tax reform proposals. They rejected the reforms, however, blaming the financial crisis on the Crown's mismanagement. Fearful of both aristocratic opposition and peasant rebellion, Louis resorted to borrowing and thus quickly doubled the size of the national debt. The monarchy appeared to have lost control of the country, and a major transformation of French society and state seemed inevitable.

Despite this ongoing turmoil, politics remained a matter of only secondary importance to Paine during the summer of 1787. He devoted his energies to lobbying the Academy of Sciences for a favorable report on his bridge project, and in August his design received an official endorsement from the academy.

Paine's travails with his beloved bridge helped cement his friendship with Jefferson and Lafayette. Both men used their considerable prestige to help promote Paine's project. The three men were regular dinner companions, spending long hours in conversation about politics and science. In early 1788, they eagerly followed the debates over the ratification of the proposed American constitution. Not surprisingly, Paine favored the new constitution, for he had always been an advocate of a strong central government. His and Jefferson's main objection was the constitutional convention's failure to include a bill of rights in the new document to protect individual liberties.

In the summer of 1788, Paine moved to England, where he spent the next 17 months trying to sell his iron bridge project. The Royal Society had declined to endorse his model, but he had heard rumors that several businessmen were interested in investing in his bridge. Although this proved to be yet another false lead, Paine wrote to Jefferson that he was certain he could raise the money for construction if he could obtain a patent. His patent application was indeed impressive, highlighting the various benefits that his iron bridge offered. Not only would it stimulate iron foundry manufacturing throughout England, but his invention made it possible to develop an export trade in bridges: The iron

Initially, Paine was very well received by French high society, but later, as he began to show compassion for the oppressed French masses and a hatred for the French monarch, Paine was looked on as a threat to the aristocracy's power and security.

Thomas Jefferson and Paine shared many political views. With respect to America's new constitution, for example, they both urged the inclusion of a bill of rights to protect individual liberties.

bridge could be manufactured in Great Britain and then erected in any part of the world.

Paine received his patent in September 1788, just a week after his initial filing. A few days later, the Walker Iron Foundry in Yorkshire agreed to construct the bridge. During the next year, Paine shuttled back and forth between London and the ironworks to check on the progress of construction. An experimental archway was completed in late April 1789, and in the spring of 1790 it was erected in the village of Paddington outside London. Paine was convinced that the bridge would bring him greater riches and fame, but this never happened: No investors came forward, and by the fall his arch had become merely a sideshow entertainment for the local population. For the charge of a shilling, visitors were allowed to walk across or jump up and down on the arch. Paine's bridge was never constructed, but his experimental design nevertheless became the prototype of the most advanced iron bridge architecture of the next century.

Paine's stay in England was not entirely devoted to his bridge project. He became friends with the members of the Society for Constitutional Reform, as well as with Mary Wollstonecraft Godwin, an early advocate of women's rights. For almost two years, Paine also acted as the unofficial American minister to England after John Adams had returned to the United States. Paine circulated among government officials and party representatives, passing full reports on English political developments to Jefferson in France. At one point, Paine even went so far as to suggest that Jefferson should discourage Congress from approving a successor to John Adams. "I know the nation well and the line of acquaintance I am in enables me to judge better than any other American can judge especially at a distance."

One of Paine's closest English associates was the noted writer and politician Edmund Burke, whom Paine had met during a visit to England in 1787. Burke was well regarded in America for having denounced King George III's policies toward the colonies. Even though he had stopped short of supporting the American War of Independence, he

was one of the few Englishmen to whom Paine referred respectfully in his writings, and Paine considered him to be a fair and generous man.

Paine and Burke spent several weeks together touring iron foundries in northern England, and Paine stayed a week at Burke's estate in Buckinghamshire. Despite their divergent political and philosophical outlooks, the two men engaged in many cordial conversations and regularly exchanged letters. While Paine was an adamant believer in republican government, Burke was a vigorous defender of the British constitutional monarchy. While Burke remained skeptical, Paine believed that major reform of the French government and society could ensure friendly relations between England and France. The subsequent course of the French Revolution would prove Paine's optimism to be unfounded and would create an irrevocable split between the two men.

During 1788 and 1789, Jefferson regularly corresponded with Paine to keep him abreast of the rapidly shifting events in revolutionary France. Widespread protest by the nobility in 1788 against restrictions on their political power had compelled Louis XVI to agree to convene a meeting of the long defunct Estates General — composed of the three orders of the nobility, clergy, and commoners — on May 1, 1789. Each group had its own interests in mind: The monarchy hoped the meeting could re-

Back in England in 1791, Paine met the writer Mary Wollstonecraft Godwin, an advocate of women's rights. At a dinner party on November 7, they discussed literature, religion, and politics. The two shared a deep hatred for the British monarchy.

The Third Estate declares itself the National Assembly of France on June 17, 1789. Though its members did not seek the dissolution of the monarchy, the new assembly was based on the liberal notion that political authority should be derived primarily from the will of the people.

solve France's financial crisis and still protect absolutist power; the aristocracy and clergy believed the Estates General could be utilized to protect their privileges and block reform; and the Third Estate — middle-class merchants, professionals, and officials — saw it as an opportunity to enact a constitutional system. During the early months of 1789, each group composed a list of grievances to be presented at the meeting. This dramatically raised the level of political consciousness among the middle class, and high public expectations about reform became widespread. Still, revolution seemed unlikely; Jefferson wrote to Paine in May that he was confident the Estates General would establish a constitutional monarchy in France.

Six weeks after the opening of the Estates General, the members of the Third Estate declared themselves the National Assembly and insisted that the other orders had no right to deliberate apart from them. The National Assembly considered their political authority to be independent of the king, and they invoked a new source of rights, the general will of the people, to justify their policies. On June 19, a majority of the clergy and some liberal nobles joined the new assembly. The next day, after discovering that their customary meeting place was locked and under guard by royal troops, the deputies of the National Assembly adjourned to a nearby tennis court. The king tried once more to send soldiers to disperse the National Assembly, but the delegates stood firm. The comte de Mirabeau, a liberal aristocrat who sided with the Third Estate, declared, "We will not move from our places here except at point of the bayonet." Louis reluctantly accepted the inevitable and invited the clergy and nobility to reassemble with the Third Estate.

The king's public compromise, however, was only a temporary retreat. In early July, Louis ordered royal regiments into Paris, ostensibly to prevent damage from public disturbances but in reality to intimidate the National Assembly. There was a growing suspicion of an aristocratic conspiracy against the National Assembly, and rumors of a military coup spread throughout the country. The Parisian masses, who had heretofore been absent from the political struggle, provided the denouement to the crisis. The *sansculottes* — shopkeepers, artisans, and wage earners — of Paris launched an insurrection on the side of the liberal reformists and in doing so brought down the state.

On July 14, 1789, a tremendous crowd stormed the Bastille, the prison that had become a hated symbol of royal oppression. The following day, Louis withdrew the troops from the capital, established a civic militia under Lafayette's leadership, and agreed to a constitutional monarchy. For Paine and Jefferson, the heroic rising of the Parisians heralded a new era of liberty, equality, and fraternity.

On August 27, 1789, the National Assembly adopted the historic Declaration of the Rights of Man and the Citizen. The first words of the document captured the motivating spirit of the French Revolution: "All men are born and remain free and equal in rights." According to the declaration, these inalienable natural rights included freedom of speech and religion, protection from imprisonment without trial or arbitrary arrest, and the sanctity of private property. Social equality was affirmed: All citizens were to be treated equally under the law, and social distinctions would now be based upon differences in talent and merit, not upon distinctions of birth.

With a tennis court serving as their meeting place, the deputies of the National Assembly take an oath of allegiance, vowing "to settle the constitution of the realm, to bring about the regeneration of public order, and to uphold the true principles of the monarchy."

However, by the fall of 1789, new rumors of aristocratic plots emerged, and in Paris a deepening economic crisis, which created severe bread shortages, intensified public dissatisfaction and fears of a counterrevolution. On October 5, a group of 7,000 women demonstrated near the Hôtel de Ville (the city hall of Paris) and then marched 12 miles to Versailles to present their grievances to the National Assembly. The women called for increased provisions for the poor masses and demanded that the king and the National Assembly move to Paris in order to become more accountable to the will of the general populace. After waiting several hours outside in the freezing rain for a response to their demands, the angry protesters burst into the royal palace. Although the crowd did not invade the king's personal chambers, the royal family was in grave danger. The following afternoon, the king agreed to return to Paris. A long procession of soldiers and protesters escorted the royal family back to the capital, where they took up residence in the long-aban-

On July 14, 1789, angry mobs stormed the fortress of the Bastille, a prison in the heart of Paris that had become a symbol of state oppression. To this day, the French commemorate the taking of the Bastille on *le quatorze juillet* each year.

doned palace of the Tuileries. Paine, hearing of the dramatic march, prepared his return to France.

Upon his arrival in France, Paine was presented with a symbolic key to the Bastille for forwarding to President Washington. He wrote to Washington that the French Revolution represented the "first ripe fruits of American principles transplanted into Europe." Indeed, Paine was convinced the Revolution marked one of the critical moments in European history. He wrote to his friend Edmund Burke that the Revolution promised to be "a forerunner of other revolutions in Europe."

Burke, however, had been horrified by the revolutionary developments in France. When he learned of the women's march on Versailles, he said: "The elements which compose human society seem all to be dissolved, and a world of monsters is to be produced in the place of it." Burke believed the French Revolution subverted the principles of sound government and posed a grave danger to England. He furiously responded to Paine's letter: "Do you mean to propose that I, who have all my life fought for the constitution, should devote the wretched remains of my days to conspire its destruction?" Burke broke off all correspondence with Paine and began work on a pamphlet to denounce the Revolution. Burke's essay, and Paine's subsequent reply, became a springboard of political debate for the next 100 years.

In October 1789, as the economic crisis in France became increasingly severe, 7,000 women marched from the Hôtel de Ville in Paris to the royal palace at Versailles to present their grievances to the king. When Paine got news of the demonstration, he returned to France.

5

"From Pole to Pole"

Paine returned to London in late March 1790. It would be eight months before Burke published his scathing indictment of the French Revolution. Paine heard of Burke's work and planned to issue a rousing defense of the Revolution to refute his arguments, so he kept close watch on the continuing developments in France.

The National Assembly did not declare France a republic. The delegates advocated the formation of a constitutional monarchy in which the king mostly deferred to the National Assembly. This political compromise appeared to win support from all sectors of French society during the first year of the Revolution.

On July 14, 1790, Lafayette staged a *fête de la fédération* in celebration of the first anniversary of the fall of the Bastille. A huge procession of the National Guard, contingents of popular militias from the provinces, and the deputies of the National Assembly were viewed by more than 400,000 people.

Your love for humanity, for liberty and equality, the useful works that have issued from your heart and pen in their defence, have determined our choice.
—letter from the National Assembly of France informing Paine that he had been elected representative of Puy-de-Dôme

---

As he had in America, Paine took up the cause of revolution in France. He called the French Revolution the "first ripe fruits of American principles transplanted into Europe." Paine, perhaps more than any writer of his day, was in tune with the intellectual underpinnings of the revolutionary period.

La Fête de la Fédération, July 14, 1790, was the first celebration of the fall of the Bastille. The French general Marquis de Lafayette staged the spectacle to garner support for the new constitutional monarchy.

Talleyrand, the bishop of Autun, celebrated mass along with 300 priests. Then, on behalf of the National Guard and citizen militia, Lafayette swore to be eternally faithful to nation, king, and constitution. Deputies of the National Assembly repeated the oath, and Louis declared: "I, King of France, swear to employ the power delegated to me in maintaining the Constitution decreed by the National Assembly, and accepted by me."

Within a year this unity, and the constitutional monarchy itself, would be completely shattered. Despite his public assertions of loyalty, the king remained secretly intransigent to reform and actively promoted counterrevolution. The majority of the aristocracy also rejected change, hoping to retain their feudal privileges. The harmony within the Third Estate was also doomed to collapse under the pressures of class divisions.

Burke's book, entitled *Reflections on the Revolution in France*, was published on November 1, 1790. An impassioned defense of privilege and the status quo, the work was a vigorous exposition of the conservative ethos: It emphasized the value of private property, the innate superiority of the ruling elite, and the mystique of royalty. He based his arguments on the assumption that all society is founded on tradition and inherited values and that to undermine these is to threaten civilized life. "To make a revolution," Burke declared, "is to subvert the ancient state of our country, and no common reasons are called to justify so violent a proceeding."

The force of Burke's position was aided considerably by his rhetorical eloquence and striking metaphors: Support for the Revolution was associated with drunkenness, and the Revolution itself was compared to a disease that was slowly eating away at the heart of the nation. Burke's portrait of the royal family was rapturously sentimental. "The age of chivalry is gone," he wrote, "and the glory of Europe is extinguished forever."

A number of reformists wrote pamphlets to refute Burke's arguments, but it was Paine's response that won the most acclaim. His pamphlet, entitled *The Rights of Man*, was published on March 16, 1791. Paine's work was less a point-by-point rebuttal of Burke's arguments than an impassioned defense of the principles of the French Revolution and republican government. Paine compared the advantages of France's revolutionary government with England's constitutional monarchy: In France, the nation and people possessed political sovereignty, whereas in England it rested with the Crown and aristocracy; the French electoral system featured broad suffrage and regular legislative elections, whereas England restricted voting to the wealthy electoral districts; France guaranteed freedom of religion and opinion, whereas England repressed dissent.

Paine provided a vivid account of the key events of the Revolution in order to correct the distorted version that Burke's "historical drama" offered. He assailed Burke's priorities, his empathy for the royal family, and his callous disregard for the struggling masses. "Not one glance of compassion, not one commiserating reflection, that I can find throughout this book has he bestowed on those who lingered out the most wretched of lives, a life without hope in the most miserable of prisons," Paine wrote.

In his book, *Reflections on the Revolution in France*, published in November 1790, the conservative politician Edmund Burke based his arguments on the value of tradition and the maintenance of the status quo. He condemned revolution as a threat to civilized life.

King Louis XVI and Queen Marie Antoinette of France lived in palatial splendor while the French people endured a long and severe economic crisis. The royal couple ignored and never really comprehended the sufferings of the masses. For example, it is alleged that when the queen was told that her subjects had no bread, she coldly responded, "Let them eat cake!"

As in *Common Sense*, Paine vigorously condemned the monarchy and hereditary privilege. The idea of hereditary legislators was "as absurd as a hereditary mathematician, or a hereditary wise man." Paine insisted further that a radical transformation of corrupt, oppressive government is justified, despite the weight of tradition.

Paine disparaged Burke's skill as a literary craftsman and ridiculed his pretentious rhetorical style. As in his American writings, in *The Rights of Man*, Paine utilized the language, images, and metaphors of the common person.

The Rights of Man became an immediate sensation. Despite government attempts to restrict circulation, the initial printing of 10,000 copies quickly sold out. Paine received numerous requests from around the country, as well as Scotland and Ireland, for permission to print a cheap edition of the book. He readily agreed to all requests, forgoing any royalties he might have received from the book. Paine's book also had a tremendous impact in the United States. With the success of his work assured, Paine returned to Paris in April 1791 to begin work on a companion volume to *The Rights of Man*.

On the morning of June 21, 1791, Paine was asleep in his bedroom when Lafayette burst in shouting, "The birds are flown." Shortly after midnight the previous day, Louis XVI, disguised as a valet, had slipped out of the Tuileries with his family and fled to the safety of the Austrian border. Despite his repeated protestations of loyalty to the Revolution, Louis had secretly attempted to enlist foreign support for the counterrevolution since 1789 and had contemplated escape on several occasions. Although Lafayette immediately alerted the National Guard and border posts upon discovering the king's flight, the royal family had been entrusted to his custody, and he feared he would be suspected of complicity in their escape. Paine was surprisingly sanguine about the king's escape. Louis's duplicity was now out in the open, thus ending all hopes for a constitutional monarchy and paving the way for a republican regime in France.

As a result of the vigilance of a village postmaster who recognized the king and blocked his passage, the royal family was captured at Varennes during the night of June 21. On the evening of June 25, they returned to Paris in what one observer called "the funeral procession of the monarchy." The king's cortege, escorted by two files of soldiers with their muskets reversed, passed through the great crowds of silent citizens lining the roadway. The king's flight to Varennes was one of the great turning points of the Revolution. It heightened the conflict between the aristocracy and the Third Estate and brought the issue of republicanism to the forefront. Until that moment, no one had dared call for an end to the monarchy, but in the next months there would be numerous appeals for the king's abdication and the establishment of a republic in France.

There was no more insistent advocate for republicanism than Paine. On July 1, his friend Achille Chastelet translated a manifesto Paine had written and printed several hundred copies to be distributed throughout Paris. The two men posted a copy of the manifesto denouncing Louis XVI on the doors of the meeting place of the National Assembly. It read, "The facts show that, if he is not a hypocrite or a traitor, he must be a madman or an imbecile . . . and in any case, entirely unfitted to discharge the function confided to him by the people." Paine's manifesto was the first public statement to demand the establishment of a French republic. He was immediately marked as a radical and condemned by members of the National Assembly.

Republican sentiment spread throughout Paris. Many of the popular political clubs and societies supported Paine's republican stance. On July 17, 1791, some 5,000 people gathered in the Champ de

Londoners take part in a fervor of activity in the courtyard of the Old Angel Inn. Paine briefly stayed at the inn while writing *The Rights of Man*, an impassioned defense of the French Revolution written mainly in response to the arguments in Burke's *Reflections*.

Mars to sign a petition supporting republican demands. A contingent of National Guard troops, led by Lafayette, unexpectedly fired upon the unarmed demonstrators, killing 12 and wounding 40 others.

The attack was another fateful episode in the history of the Revolution. From that moment on, the Third Estate was irrevocably split between supporters of the constitutional monarchy and the republicans. The incident had far-reaching consequences abroad as well. On August 27, 1791, the Declaration of Pillnitz was signed by the Holy Roman Emperor Leopold II and King Frederick William II of Prussia, threatening the Revolution with armed intervention should the monarchy be overthrown. Within France, war had become the final recourse for the aristocracy and monarchy. "Instead of a civil war, there will be a foreign war," Louis wrote secretly on December 14, 1791, "and things will be much the better for it." A war between revolutionary France and the nations of the monarchies of Europe now seemed inevitable.

Paine returned to London in early July 1791 a celebrity. *The Rights of Man* was still selling

The French royal family is escorted from Varennes back to Paris by armed guards. Louis XVI's failed attempt to flee prompted numerous calls for the dissolution of the French monarchy. Paine and a significant portion of the French citizenry hoped that the monarchy would eventually be replaced with a republican government.

The London bookseller Thomas Cleo Rickman was Paine's friend and the publisher of the second part of *The Rights of Man*. Under severe criticism and the threat of criminal prosecution for publishing Paine's work, Rickman left London for Paris.

strongly and it seemed as if every London newspaper featured a daily article, story or editorial on Paine — most of them unfavorable. Yet among the working population, especially the members of the political societies that supported the French Revolution and the reformers of the English system, Paine's popularity was never greater. "I have got the ear of the country," he said. "I shall go on and at least show them, what is a novelty here, that there can be a person beyond the reach of corruption."

During the fall, Paine spent most of his time writing and visiting the political clubs. In November, he attended a meeting of the Revolution Society in London; among the toasts made that evening was one to "Mr. Paine, with thanks for his defense of the rights of man," to which Paine toasted "the Revolution of the world!" Despite increasing government pressure against radicals, Paine remained a steadfast supporter of the Revolution. "We have truth on our side," he said, "the French Revolution opens to the world an opportunity in which all good citizens must rejoice — that of promoting the general happiness of man."

Paine published the second part of *The Rights of Man* in February 1792. He again provided a devastating critique of the monarchy and the defects of England's political institutions. Poverty, corruption, and discontent persisted in British society, he claimed, because the English government failed to provide for its people. One cannot expect this outmoded government to act otherwise, he stated, for its officials were merely representatives of special interests. This is why, he wrote, revolution "may be considered the order of the day." "If universal peace, civilization, and commerce are ever to be the happy lot of man," he said, "it cannot be accomplished but by a revolution in their system of governments."

Paine not only asserted the superiority of republican government but also offered a breathtaking vision of how a republican government could begin to ameliorate poverty within England. He proposed a series of public policies — progressive income taxes, government grants to the poor for education and housing, unemployment relief and public jobs, maternity grants and child allowances, and old age pensions. He insisted that his program was not a utopian pipe dream but could be accomplished if the government simply stopped fighting foreign wars and ended its financial support of the aristocracy. The needs of the many, Paine argued, could be satisfied if the selfishness of the privileged few was constrained.

The second part of *The Rights of Man* became the best-selling book in British history. Within one year, 200,000 copies were either sold or distributed free in a country with a population of little more than 10 million (this would be equivalent to selling 5 million copies in the United States today). *The Rights of Man* represented a critical turning point in the history of British radicalism; Paine's writings became the dividing line that separated reformists from revolutionaries.

Artisans and journeymen, unable to vote or join unions, flocked to new radical societies, such as the London Corresponding Society. Though Paine's

Members of a radical political society meet in a London house. The publication of *The Rights of Man* stimulated the political climate in England during the 1790s and to some degree prompted the formation of many such societies.

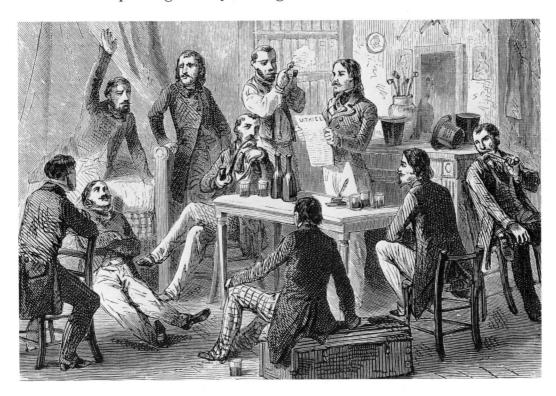

writing alone did not create this vibrant political climate (the American and French revolutions had already stimulated demands for reform in Britain), it did offer British radicals a compelling political vision that explained not only why social and political inequities were so prevalent but also how they could be eradicated. Paine won great renown and popularity within the radical societies. Workers in Sheffield, for instance, wrote new lyrics to the tune of the national anthem:

God save great Thomas Paine
 His 'Rights of Man' to explain
  to every soul.
 He makes the blind to see
 What dupes and slaves they be
 And points out liberty
  from pole to pole.

By the spring of 1792, the British government was haunted by the specter of revolution at home and war abroad. The Pitt government launched a widespread crackdown on the popular movement. Mobs were funded and organized to attack the homes of radical leaders who spoke in favor of the French Revolution. Government spies, agents, and provocateurs infiltrated many of the radical societies. The government's main target, however, was Paine. Prime Minister William Pitt stated that *The Rights of Man* "perverted all men's minds" and would lead to "the total subversion of the established form of government." On May 21, a royal proclamation was issued to prevent the publication of "wicked and seditious writings," and although it did not mention Paine by name, the order was clearly referring to his work.

The English government sponsored the publication of a slanderous biography of Paine and encouraged the formation of Loyalist clubs, which published anti-Paine pamphlets and cartoons. Paine was hung in effigy countless times, and one of the more popular songs on those occasions was "Old Satan had a darling boy/Full equal he to Cain/Both peace and order to destroy/His name was Thomas Paine."

England's prime minister William Pitt condemned Paine's work as subversive. In 1792, Paine, by then a pariah in England for his radical polemics, spent a brief period in the countryside, where he concentrated on his writing and occasionally visited with close friends.

During the late 18th century, tokens were often distributed to disseminate political propaganda. The top three coins — one depicting "The Wrongs of Man," another showing Paine hanging from the gallows, and yet another referring to "the knave of Jacobin clubs" — were minted to discredit Paine. The bottom two were distributed by one of Paine's supporters, publisher Thomas Spence.

In June, Paine was indicted on charges of sedition for the publication of *The Rights of Man*. He spent most of the summer in quiet isolation — writing, strolling through the countryside, and dining with his close friends. In August, the French revolutionaries made Paine an honorary French citizen, and he was invited by the department of Calais to serve as its representative to the National Convention, which would convene in September to begin formulating a new constitution for the French republic. Given his worsening legal predicament and the growing repression of radicals, Paine decided to accept the offer. He prepared for his departure in his accustomed leisurely fashion, but he was forced to accelerate his timetable due to rumors of his imminent arrest. On the evening of September 13, 1792, Paine boarded a ship for France; it was the last time he would set foot in his native England.

6

Citizen Paine

After his triumphant reception at Calais, Paine went to Paris to participate in the opening of the National Convention. Paine was very well received: A number of deputies rose and applauded his entrance, and many greeted him personally and shook his hand.

The political situation in France had changed radically since Paine's last visit, in July 1791. In April 1792, under the leadership of Paine's friend Jacques-Pierre Brissot and other members of a political group known as the Girondins, the National Assembly declared war on Austria. Brissot demanded that the Revolution, as a "war of the human race against its oppressors," be extended to all the nations in Europe. Opposed to this idea was Maximilien Robespierre, a lawyer representing the Paris sectors in the assembly and the leader of the assembly's other major political group, the Jacobins. He implored the Assembly, "Restore order in your own house, before you carry liberty elsewhere."

I think it necessary that Louis XVI should be tried . . . because this measure appears to me just, lawful, and conformable to sound policy. If Louis is innocent, let us put him to prove his innocence.
—THOMAS PAINE
excerpt from a paper read to the convention, November 21, 1792

In 1792, Paine was made an honorary French citizen and invited to attend the French National Convention as a representative from Calais. He left for France that September just in time to avoid being arrested by English authorities.

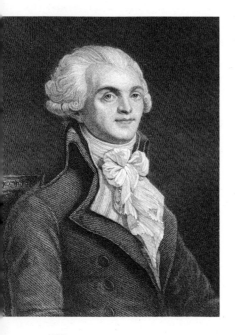

Maximilien Robespierre, lawyer and leader of the Jacobins, was the chief political spokesman for France's oppressed working class during France's revolutionary period. He adopted a highly moral stance derived from the ideals of the Enlightenment philosophers, urging France to strive toward a "republic of virtue."

The war with Austria and Prussia had a powerful impact on the French social and political sphere in that it helped bring about the downfall of the monarchy by exposing the king's double-dealing, and it in effect transformed the sansculottes into a powerful pressure group. With their greater leverage, the sansculottes demanded price controls to relieve the economic problems brought on by the war and insisted on greater autonomy from the National Assembly for local political authorities. These demands created a conflict between the sansculottes and the French political establishment, dominated by the Girondins and Jacobins, who, in turn, were split over how to respond to these demands.

In the early summer of 1792, the economic situation in France worsened, and the French army reeled from a series of devastating defeats. In July, as Prussian troops crossed the border into France, the National Assembly declared a state of emergency. Fears of a counterrevolutionary coup d'état were rampant. On August 10, 1792, sansculottes and members of the National Guard, armed with pitchforks and muskets, united under the direction of the newly formed revolutionary Paris Commune and stormed the Tuileries, forcing the king to seek refuge in the National Assembly. The king was imprisoned a week later, and on September 21, the National Convention voted to establish a republican constitution for France — in effect ending the monarchy. After an aborted attempt to rouse his troops to march on Paris and disband the National Assembly, Lafayette abandoned the Revolution and defected to the Austrian side on August 19. Other aristocrats and supporters of the constitutional monarchy joined the swelling ranks of émigrés in the fall.

It was during this crisis that the National Convention began. Paine, who at 55 was one of the oldest deputies in the convention, did not play a major part in its proceedings. He had never learned to read or speak French, so he mostly associated with the English and Irish émigrés living in Paris or with Frenchmen such as Brissot and Condorcet, who spoke fluent English. Paine's friendship with the

Girondin leaders was also based on their common belief in international revolution and their shared vision of the American Revolution. Yet, because his personal relations were restricted mostly to foreigners and aristocratic republicans, Paine did not develop ties with the sansculottes, and this severely limited his perception of events. Also, Paine never stopped viewing the French Revolution through the lens of the American Revolution and thus never realized important differences between the two struggles.

Paine, who also had no firsthand experience in the process of governing, was out of his depth when it came to the politics of the convention. He always considered himself above party politics, and he had a similar disdain for the factional disputes between the Jacobins and Girondins. Paine had no tolerance for the bitter infighting that characterized party debates within the convention, nor was he temperamentally suited to the daily grind of governing. Paine's friend Jeanne-Marie Roland, commonly known simply as Madame Roland, admired his original and bold writing style, but admitted he was "better at lighting the way for Revolution" than in making one.

With the economic situation in France at a terrible low, a violent insurrection erupted on August 10, 1792. In an attempt to force the king's abdication, sansculottes and members of the National Guard stormed the Tuileries, the Paris residence of the royal family.

Louis, his family, and other members of the monarchical bureaucracy were imprisoned as the revolutionary tide in France swelled in 1792. Here, French aristocrats try to ease each other's anxiety while awaiting their fate.

The convention was colored by the ongoing, bitter contest between the Jacobins and Girondins. The Girondins considered the Jacobins dangerous egalitarians who would destroy all distinctions in society, whereas the Jacobins, headed by Robespierre, Jean-Paul Marat, and Georges-Jacques Danton, attacked the Girondins for being more concerned with satisfying their own private interests than the needs of the people.

The event that most dominated the convention's attention, and the Jacobin-Girondin rivalry as well, was the debate over whether Louis XVI should be tried for his crimes against the people. The debate over the king's fate began in early November. The 25-year-old Jacobin leader Louis-Antoine Saint-Just was one of the first prominent orators. He insisted that the very question of a trial itself was a mistaken notion; the key issue before the convention was not to try the king but to accomplish a political act that would further the Revolution. Louis was not a defendant, Saint-Just insisted, but an enemy of France and therefore should suffer the consequences. After several weeks of debate, the convention was stunned when incriminating documents were discovered in a safe in the king's former residence in the Tuileries. The documents showed that while he was pledging his loyalty to the constitutional monarchy, Louis was urging foreign powers to invade France and reestablish the absolute monarchy. As the evidence of this treachery came to light, it was clear that Louis would have to stand trial.

On November 21, Paine addressed the convention and expressed his agreement that the king should be tried. The trial of the king, Paine urged, should not be an act of revenge but a useful demonstration of "the necessity of Revolutions." Paine believed that Louis should be treated in a compassionate manner that would reflect well on the Revolution. Robespierre delivered the decisive speech on December 1. Echoing Saint-Just's remarks, Robespierre argued that the convention was not a court sitting in judgment but a legislature that had a duty to protect the gains of the Revolution. "You have not to pronounce a verdict for or against a man, but to adopt a measure of public safety, to perform an act of rational foresight," Robespierre exclaimed. "Louis must die because France must live."

On January 14, 1793, the public galleries of the convention were packed to capacity. Three questions were submitted for the deputies' deliberation: First, was Louis guilty of conspiring against the people; second, should the verdict of the convention be referred to the people for ratification; and third, what punishment should Louis receive? To decide the issue, each deputy addressed the convention in his turn.

Chaos reigns as men of diverse political persuasions compete for the floor at the French National Convention. Paine had neither the patience nor the desire to take part in the bitter infighting that characterized French politics during the revolutionary period.

The following day, Paine made a statement to the convention with the help of a translator. "I submit my proposal as an American who feels a debt of gratitude he owes to every Frenchman," Paine declared. "I submit it as a man, who albeit an adversary of kings, forgets not that they are subject to human frailties." After reviewing the sordid history of the monarchy, Paine agreed that Louis deserved to be tried so that the extent of his treachery and corruption would become public knowledge.

To counter the numerous Jacobin deputies who had called for the king's execution, Paine shrewdly reminded the convention of a speech Robespierre had delivered earlier to the National Assembly, calling for the abolition of the death penalty. "This cause must find its advocates in every corner where enlightened politicians and lovers of humanity exist," he said, "and it ought above all to find them in this assembly." Paine argued that since France was the first European nation to abolish the monarchy, it should also be the first to abolish capital punishment.

Paine reminded the deputies of the support that France, under Louis's reign, had granted to the American Revolution. As a citizen of both countries, he therefore boldly suggested banishing Louis to the United States. "There, remote from the miseries and crimes of royalty, he may learn," Paine said, "that the true system of government consists not in monarchs, but in fair, equal and honorable representation." He suggested that Louis and his family be detained in prison until the end of the war and then exiled permanently from France. Paine's address was a masterpiece, marvelously interweaving moral and practical appeals. On January 15, the convention passed judgment on the first two questions. Louis was unanimously declared guilty of conspiracy; the proposal to submit the decision to the people was rejected. Paine sided with the majority on both questions.

The debate on the third critical question, whether Louis should be executed, imprisoned, or banished, started on January 16. Voting began in the evening and lasted until the following night. Each of the

Madame Roland, whose salon became a political center for republicans and the Girondins, was a close friend of Paine's and attested to his disdain for practical politics and his preference for devising political theories and systems.

deputies announced his vote at the central podium, usually with a simple statement, sometimes with a long speech. The public gallery was again filled with spectators who kept a tally on large blackboards, hissing or cheering as each vote was recorded. Some deputies were intimidated by the raucous crowd and were afraid to be seen as moderates by their vote.

The influential independent deputy Bertrand Barère voted for the death penalty, stating: "As a classical author said, the tree of liberty grows only when it is watered by the blood of all species of tyrants. The law says death, and I am only its voice." Paine proclaimed, "I vote for the detention of Louis until the end of the war, and after that his perpetual banishment." Many delegates specifically cited Paine's example, casting their votes against Louis's execution. "By the example of Thomas Paine, whose vote is not suspect," said one delegate, "by the example of that illustrious stranger, friend of the people, enemy of kings and royalty, and zealous defender of republican liberty, I vote for imprisonment during the war, and banishment at peace." In the final vote, 361 deputies voted unconditionally for death, 26 voted for death with an appeal for clemency, and 334 voted in favor of imprisonment or exile. By a majority of one, the convention fatefully ordered the death of the king.

The next day, a number of Girondin deputies called for a stay of execution for Louis, and another acrimonious debate ensued. A member of the convention, Jean-Henri Bancal, read Paine's prepared speech in French translation. A few moments after the speech began, Marat jumped to his feet and loudly protested that Paine should be prohibited from speaking on this issue because his religious principles as a Quaker were opposed to capital punishment. Marat's interruption precipitated a huge commotion in the convention. Still, Paine stood quietly. Some deputies were unsure of what it meant to be a Quaker; others insisted that Paine's freedom of speech should be recognized and his views should be heard. It was obvious that Marat was concerned that Paine's enormous prestige might sway the

Georges-Jacques Danton, lawyer and leader of the radical Cordelier Club, was a staunch defender of the French poor. He used his powerful oratorical skills to sway and intensify public opinion against the monarchy, and he played an important role in the provisional government after the abdication of the king.

closely divided convention. After a few moments, the uproar gradually subsided, and Bancal continued with Paine's speech.

"My language has always been that of liberty and humanity," Paine wrote, "and I knew by experience that nothing so excites a nation as the union of these two principles, under all circumstances." Paine was afraid that future historians would not look kindly on the convention's death sentence on the king, that "what today seems an act of justice may then appear as an act of vengeance." Paine was concerned that Louis's execution might seriously jeopardize France's relations with the United States; he believed that the king's death would inevitably "spread universal sorrow." "If on my return to America, I should employ myself in a history of the French Revolution," he said, "I had rather record a thousand errors dictated by humanity, than one inspired by a justice too severe."

Marat interrupted a second time and told the convention, "I denounce the interpreter, and I maintain that such is not the opinion of Thomas Paine. It is a wicked and faithless translation." A member of

The National Convention deliberates over the fate of Louis XVI in January 1793. Paine (third row, fourth from right, wearing hat), who believed that Louis's execution would reflect badly on the Revolution, pleaded with the tribunal to spare the deposed king's life.

the convention who had seen Paine's original statement vouched for the accuracy of the translation. The deputy finished reading Paine's statement, at which time Marat rose for a third time and cried out that Paine had only voted against the death sentence because he was a Quaker. "I voted against it," Paine replied directly, "both morally and politically." Paine's impassioned words had little effect on the convention's outcome. On January 20, the convention voted 380 to 310 that Louis was to be executed within 24 hours. The next morning, Louis XVI died under the guillotine.

The head of Louis XVI is displayed before a jeering crowd of French soldiers and citizens on January 20, 1793, as his body is removed from the guillotine. Despite Paine's skills in the art of persuasion, the National Convention voted by a majority of one to execute the king.

7

The Terror

The National Convention declared war against England and the United Provinces of the Netherlands on February 1, 1793. Paine was still optimistic about the future of the Revolution: "The tyrants of the earth are leagued against France; but with little effect. Although single handed and alone, she still stands unshaken, unsubdued, and undaunted," Paine said.

As long as the revolutionary armies held an advantage on the battlefield, the Girondins were able to maintain control of the convention. However, the situation at home shifted dramatically in March: A counterrevolutionary rebellion broke out in the Vendée, a western province of France, against the mandatory nationwide draft; a small group of extreme revolutionaries staged an insurrection in Paris; the economy once again deteriorated; and, as prices soared and essential supplies became increasingly scarce, opposition to the Girondins' economic policies intensified.

They have nothing against me—except that they do not choose I should be in a state of freedom to write my mind freely upon things I have seen.
—THOMAS PAINE
while incarcerated in Luxembourg prison

Robespierre assumed dictatorial powers in France in July 1793 and sent tens of thousands to the guillotine for what he believed was the sake of saving the Revolution. Ultimately, he would meet his own fate under the guillotine's swift blade.

On April 5, the Jacobin leader Marat sent an address to the Paris section warning of an impending counterrevolution. He stated that unless the "nest of traitors" was removed from the convention, a dictatorship would be needed to preserve the Revolution. Although the Girondins were not specifically mentioned, Marat's remarks were clearly directed at them, and they in turn seized the opportunity to use Marat's inflammatory rhetoric to bolster their dwindling power in the convention. On April 12, the convention, at the urging of the Girondin deputies, declared that Marat should be tried for plotting to overthrow the convention.

Paine, who had no personal dealings with Marat, inadvertently became embroiled in the controversy. After Marat's outburst, his roommate, a young English doctor named William Johnson, inexplicably thought Paine's life was in danger and in his dejection decided to commit suicide. (He stabbed himself but was hurt only slightly.) In his suicide note, Johnson condemned Marat: "I came to France in order to enjoy liberty, but it has been assassinated by Marat. . . . I cannot endure the doleful spectacle of the eruption of imbecility and inhumanity over talent and virtue." The Girondins seized upon this incident as a way to impugn Marat's character, and, with Paine's permission, they published a copy of the suicide note in the Paris press. Their ploy backfired, however.

Marat's impeachment trial, supposedly an investigation into his treasonous behavior, instead became an indictment of the Girondins for trying to exploit the Johnson incident for their own political advantage. Numerous witnesses testified that Johnson's behavior was abnormal, and Johnson himself admitted in court that his affection for Paine had motivated his misguided actions. Paine was also called as a witness, and he stated that he believed Johnson had attempted suicide because he feared he would be denounced by Marat. At this point Marat interrupted and said that it was not Johnson but Paine whom he had intended to denounce. The issues that had brought about Marat's prosecution in the first place were lost in the confusion, so Marat

was acquitted by the tribunal. His supporters triumphantly carried him out of the courtroom and through the streets of Paris to the National Convention, where he delivered a fiery speech condemning the traitors of the Revolution. After Marat's assassination in July, any opponent of the martyred Jacobin leader became suspect, and Paine's role in the trial was not forgotten.

In late April, the convention was presented with a petition, signed by numerous Parisians, demanding the expulsion and arrest of 22 deputies. All of the persons named were affiliated with the Girondin wing, and many of Paine's closest friends, including Brissot and Condorcet, were on the list. Paine's name was conspicuously missing; his prestige was still strong enough that the sansculottes considered him to be above petty factions. The convention dismissed the petition, but it marked a critical stage in Paine's attitude toward the Revolution.

The sansculottes' initiative was clearly inspired, if not organized, by the Jacobin leadership, and Paine was fearful of the Revolution being dominated

In June 1793, Girondins leave the convention hall with their hands raised to signify their solidarity despite having just fallen from power. Within a year most of the Girondin leaders were either imprisoned, hiding, or dead.

Believing she was avenging imprisoned Girondins, the French noblewoman Charlotte Corday leaves the Jacobin leader Jean-Paul Marat to die in his bath after stabbing him in July 1793. When Corday, sentenced to death for committing the murder, approached the scaffold and found her view of the guillotine blocked by her considerate executioner, she objected, "Please, I have a right to be curious. I have never seen one before."

by men "who act without either prudence or morality." With his perceptions irrevocably shaped by the American Revolution, Paine could only envision a revolution progressing by constitutional means. He disapproved of the sansculottes' method of political participation through crowd activity, and he believed the Jacobins' support of the sansculottes would only foster further divisiveness. Paine wrote to Jefferson, "Had this Revolution been conducted consistently with its principles, there was once a good prospect of extending liberty through the greatest part of Europe, but now I relinquish that hope."

The Revolution took a radical turn in June because of yet another fateful intervention by the Parisian sansculottes. From May 31 to June 2, the Paris sections formed a new revolutionary committee, with an expanded National Guard made up of a revolutionary militia of sansculottes. The sansculottes seized key positions throughout the city, and on June 2, National Guard contingents surrounded the convention hall and demanded the arrest of the Girondin leaders. It was at this moment that Paine attempted to enter the hall. Fortunately, he was stopped outside by Danton, who warned Paine that he would be risking arrest by entering. Paine told Danton that perhaps Pierre Vergniaud (a deputy in the convention) was right when he predicted that the French Revolution, like the Roman god Saturn, would devour its own children. Danton shrugged his shoulders and replied: "Revolutions cannot be made with rosewater."

Inside the convention, the deputies voted to disregard the National Guard's ultimatum and decided to march as a group past the troops guarding the hall. As some deputies attempted to leave, they were told by the commander of the sansculottes that his troops would open fire unless they returned to their seats. The deputies acquiesced in the sansculottes' demands and voted to suspend and imprison the accused Girondins, who were placed under house arrest. The "moral insurrection of the people," as Robespierre termed the uprising, was the final blow to the Girondins. Within the year, most of their leaders were either dead, imprisoned, or in hiding.

The June insurrection also represented the final step in the Jacobins' rise to power. In July, Robespierre and his principal lieutenants joined the Committee of Public Safety, which had been formed in April. Up to this point, the committee had been an ineffectual agency, but the needs of war and public order compelled Robespierre and his associates to transform it into the core of a strong central government. From July 1793 to July 1794, the Committee of Public Safety assumed extensive dictatorial powers over diplomacy, the war, the national economy, and general policy (an auxiliary Committee of General Security was responsible for the police and internal security). The 12 members of the committee, all of whom were under 40 years of age, shared in directing policy and conducting the war, but Robespierre clearly emerged as the preeminent member.

The first priority of the revolutionary government was to revitalize the nation's war effort. In August,

Citizens storm a printer's shop in order to gain access to news of the day's events during the Reign of Terror. Robespierre's revolutionary government severely limited private enterprise and placed tight controls on speech and the press.

the committee decreed a *levée en masse*, a mobilization of the entire nation for the war. Young men were drafted to serve in the revolutionary armies, with women, children, and the elderly providing assistance behind the lines. State workshops were formed to manufacture weapons. Jacobin leaders visited the front to bolster the troops' morale and to ensure the adequacy of their supplies. By the spring of 1794, the revolutionary armies totaled over 1 million men, and the tide of battle turned in France's favor. The revolutionary troops quelled the domestic uprisings and drove the enemy forces across the borders.

Marie Antoinette was led to the guillotine in October 1793, blinded by the light of day, which she had not seen during her many months in a dark Paris prison. When she accidentally stepped on the executioner's foot, she said to him, "Forgive me. I did not do it on purpose."

The requirements of the war and pressures from the sansculottes combined to convince the committee to adopt severe economic measures. The government requisitioned all material resources, limiting the freedom of private enterprise; placed tight controls over prices, wages, and profits; nationalized key industries relating to defense; and confiscated the properties of suspected counterrevolutionaries. The Jacobins' social program represented a victory for the sansculottes; in return for their support of the Jacobin cause, they achieved greater economic security and increased participation in political affairs.

To secure their social program at home and military victory abroad, the Committee of Public Safety resorted to the use of the guillotine against its opponents. During the Reign of Terror, as this period is known to history, the beheading of political foes became official state policy. It was particularly severe in areas where counterrevolutionary armed rebellion was most widespread. To the extent that terror made it possible to impose a controlled economy or defeat the counterrevolution, it was a decisive factor for military victory, and it is doubtful that the Republic could have survived without it. Yet, the Reign of Terror also significantly perverted the atmosphere of the Revolution; it poisoned all relations with mutual suspicion and recrimination and marked the end of any popular democracy in the Revolution.

On October 3, the 22 Girondin leaders were brought before the National Convention and officially accused as traitors to the Revolution. Several Jacobin deputies denounced and called for the arrest of the 73 representatives, including Paine, who had voted against the expulsion of the Girondins back in June. Paine, an Englishman, was singled out as a threat, given that France was currently at war with England. On October 31, two weeks after the execution of Marie Antoinette, Louis XVI's widow, Paine's Girondin friends were carted off to the guillotine in the place de la Révolution.

Paine did not witness any of these incidents. He stayed at his home in virtual isolation after the June

Girondin leaders Brissot, Vergniaud, Gensonne, and others are led to the guillotine at the place de la Révolution in Paris. As Paine watched many of his Girondin friends carted off to their death, he began to suspect that his own execution was imminent.

uprising, drinking heavily to relieve his growing anxiety and despair. "I went little to the Convention," he later wrote, "and then only to make my appearance; because I found it impossible to join in their tremendous decrees, and useless and dangerous to oppose them." Paine's vote and impassioned speech against the execution of the king, coupled with his intimate friendships with the Girondins, branded him as an enemy of the Revolution. It was an extremely harrowing period for Paine. "I saw most of my intimate friends destroyed, others daily carried to prison," he said, "and I had reason to believe and had also intimations given me that some danger was approaching myself."

On December 28, 1793, Paine was awakened at 4:00 A.M. by a pounding on his door. Two officers from the Committee of General Security, accompanied by five policemen, entered the room and informed Paine that he was under arrest and that his papers were to be confiscated. Paine was in the midst of completing a new essay, which later became his great work *The Age of Reason*, and he was anxious to safeguard the manuscript. Paine informed the officers that his papers were located at the house of his friend Joel Barlow; he felt if another American were present when his papers were examined, perhaps his manuscript could be saved. The police escorted him to Barlow's house, examined his papers, and decided that there was nothing suspicious. By the early afternoon, Paine was led off to Luxembourg Prison.

It appeared that the length of Paine's stay in prison hinged upon the question of his citizenship. Paine asserted that, despite his birth in England, he had become an American by virtue of participating in the American Revolution. If the United States government strongly supported Paine's claim of citizenship, it was likely that his release could be secured. France, at war with the nations of Europe, could ill afford to jeopardize its friendly relations with the United States. Unfortunately, the American minister to France at the time was Gouverneur Morris, who had a long-standing personal and political antipathy to Paine. The two men had clashed at the time of the Deane affair, and Morris had always been contemptuous of Paine's radicalism. Morris made only a halfhearted attempt to get Paine released. He wrote a perfunctory note to the minister of foreign affairs, asking for information about Paine's arrest, and was told that Paine had renounced his American citizenship when he became a deputy in the National Convention. Morris never forcefully pressed the case for Paine's citizenship and merely advised Paine to keep a low profile in prison.

Paine was quite fortunate to have been confined in Luxembourg Prison. The other 12 prisons in Paris were overcrowded and plagued by disease. At Luxembourg, a former palace renovated to accommodate up to 1,000 prisoners, conditions were luxurious by comparison: Prisoners lived in small communal groups, doing their own cooking and cleaning; and the warden kept relaxed security. Indeed, because of its easy visitation policy in which

> *His cheerful philosophy under the certain expectation of death, his sensibility of heart, his brilliant powers of conversation . . . rendered him a very general favorite with his companions in misfortune.*
> —fellow inmate of Paine's at Luxembourg

male and female inmates mingled regularly, the prison earned a reputation as the largest brothel in Paris. Paine, believing the government had imprisoned him to prevent him from swaying public opinion in America against the Revolution, did not fear for his life. "They have nothing against me," he wrote, "except they do not choose I should be in a state of freedom to write my mind freely upon things I have seen." Paine's sense of security vanished, however, once the Reign of Terror entered its extreme phase in the spring of 1794.

The Jacobins' extermination of their right- and left-wing opposition in March led to more violence that summer. In June, after an attempted assassination of Robespierre, the National Convention passed a new law that deprived prisoners of the right to counsel and compelled judges to render verdicts of either acquittal or death. The ensuing 47 days were horrific beyond anyone's imagination. More than 1,000 Parisians were guillotined during this period, 100 more than had been executed in the preceding 16 months, and the killing became increasingly arbitrary, as ordinary citizens were executed for no reason. The entire city was caught in a web of fear and hatred.

Conditions inside Luxembourg Prison also worsened that summer. No prisoner could count on his life past 24 hours, and each night the prison corridors echoed with the cries of men being sent to the guillotine. On one night in particular, 168 inmates were guillotined. "Many a man whom I have passed an hour with in conversation I have seen marching to his destruction the next hour," Paine wrote years later. "For what rendered the scene more horrible was that they were generally taken away at midnight, so that every man went to bed with the apprehension of never seeing his friends or the world again."

Paine escaped the guillotine purely by chance. Each evening, the guards chalked a cross on the doors of the prisoners who were scheduled to be executed. One night, Paine left his cell door opened outwards and the guards mistakenly placed the chalk mark on the inside of his door. When Paine

The American statesman Gouverneur Morris. When Paine was imprisoned in December 1793, Morris, then the American minister to France, remembered his differences with Paine over the Deane affair and made virtually no effort to effect his release.

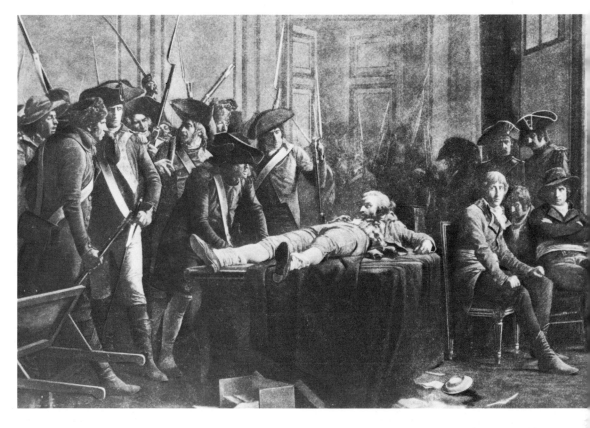

and his roommates returned to their cell, they shut their door for the night, so the mark went unobserved. When the guards made their midnight rounds, they fortuitously passed by Paine's cell.

Despite these terrifying conditions, Paine's courage impressed his fellow inmates. As the historian David Hawke recounts, one prisoner spoke fondly about Paine: "His cheerful philosophy under the certain expectation of death, his sensibility of heart, his brilliant powers of conversation, and his sportive vein of wit, rendered him a very general favorite with his companions of misfortune, who found a refuge from evil in the charms of his society. He was the confidant of the unhappy, the counselor of the perplexed, and to his sympathizing friendship, many a devoted victim in the hour of death confided the last creases of humanity, and the last wishes of tenderness." Eventually, Paine collapsed under the strain of prison life and fell seriously ill. He was

Robespierre is interrogated following his suicide attempt. The night before his scheduled execution, Robespierre tried to cheat the executioner by taking his own life with a pistol, but the bullet merely shattered his jawbone.

cared for by two inmate doctors, but for five weeks Paine lay in his bed incoherent and unaware of events inside or outside the prison. He regained consciousness in early July to learn that the Jacobin revolutionary government had fallen and that Robespierre and his followers had been executed.

The Jacobins' intensification of the Reign of Terror in the spring had hastened their own downfall. In the wake of the repression of the Left opposition, the sansculottes' revolutionary committees and popular societies were disbanded, and popular enthusiasm for the revolutionary government waned. The Jacobins' successful conduct of the war and suppression of the internal rebellion paradoxically subverted support for their government. Once military victory was assured and the danger of popular insurrection had passed, there was no longer any need for the independent deputies of the National Convention to countenance a government based on a policy of terror. Severe personality clashes and disagreements within the Committee of Public Safety itself also contributed to the Jacobins' demise. On July 10, Robespierre and his colleagues were sent to the guillotine without a trial. It marked the culmination of the Revolution.

Ten days after Robespierre's death, Paine sent a letter to the government appealing for his release from prison. "My friends, 8 months' loss of liberty," he wrote, "seems almost a lifetime to a man who has been the unceasing defender of liberty for 20 years." He pointed out that he had made huge personal sacrifices during the past seven years "in hope of seeing a Revolution happily established in France, that might serve as a model to the rest of Europe." Paine blamed the Jacobins for betraying this dream but maintained that he felt no vindictiveness toward the French government. The only thing he wanted now was a speedy resolution of his case and his release from jail.

Paine's chances for freedom improved immeasurably with the appointment in August of James Monroe as the new American minister to France. Paine wrote Monroe in September, describing the horrendous ordeal he had suffered through in the

Take from mine the hardest, roughest stone,/It needs no fashion, it is WASHINGTON./ But if you chisel, let your strokes be rude,/And on his breast engrave ingratitude.
—THOMAS PAINE
quatrain written out of anguish over Washington's alleged indifference to his imprisonment

past year and urging him to devote his full efforts to securing his release. At age 57, Paine, in terms of both age and time served, was nearly the oldest inhabitant of Paris's prisons, and he worried that he might spend the rest of his life in jail. "There is now a moment of calm," Paine exclaimed, "but I am not out of danger till I am out of prison." Monroe fully accepted Paine's claim to American citizenship. He wrote to Paine that "by being with us through the revolution, you are of our country, as absolutely as if you had been born there." With Monroe's intervention, Paine left Luxembourg Prison on November 4, 1794, almost 10 months since the day of his arrest. Paine's historic sojourn in the French Revolution had come to a close.

Robespierre (with bandaged jaw) and his associates are executed on July 28, 1794. The French people took revenge on Robespierre, who, during his Reign of Terror, had ordered the execution of some 40,000 alleged counterrevolutionaries, approximately 28,000 of whom were peasants and laborers.

TREASON
ANARCHY MURDER
EQUALITY MADNESS
CRUELTY
MISERY
FAMINE
NATIONAL & PRIVATE RUIN
INGRATITUDE IDLENESS
TREACHERY
INJUSTICE
RIGHTS of MAN
Common Nonsense
Equality of Property
&c &c
Loyalty
Magna Charta
National Prosperity
Religion
Morality
Obedience to the Laws
Industry
Personal Security
Justice
Inheritance

8
The Twilight Years

Monroe invited Paine to stay as a guest in his house after his release from prison. Paine was in poor physical condition as a result of his ordeal, but even so, a few days later he was again on the streets of Paris. In December, the decree prohibiting foreigners from serving as deputies in the National Convention was repealed, and Paine was readmitted to the assembly. Still, for the next six months, Paine stayed in seclusion — writing and recovering his strength. He considered returning to America, but he was still a wanted felon in England and did not want to risk capture by the British. Considering British naval dominance, any sea journey would have been perilous.

When Paine resumed his position within the convention, it was obvious that there had been a dramatic conservative reaction against Jacobin rule. The convention proposed a new system of government that sharply curtailed democratic participation. The constitution of 1795 replaced universal suffrage, or voting rights for all citizens, with a sys-

> *His words, be they truths or errors, take on life, and work their good or evil to all generations.*
> —ERIC FONER
> Paine biographer, on Paine

When Paine was released from prison, he was in poor physical condition and was well out of favor with the political leaders then holding the reigns of power. Still, he published some of his best work in the years that followed, including *The Age of Reason*.

tem of election requiring property ownership for voting and holding office. Paine returned to the convention in June, his first visit since the fall of the Girondins two years earlier, to denounce the new constitution as a betrayal of the original principles of the Revolution. "In my opinion, if you subvert the basis of Revolution, if you dispense with principles," he said, "and substitute expedients, you will extinguish that enthusiasm and energy which have hitherto been the life and soul of the Revolution, and you will substitute in its place nothing but a cold self-interest." Paine reaffirmed his support for universal suffrage and republicanism, but his courageous words fell on deaf ears. The new constitution was approved, and the convention was replaced by a new legislative body and a five-member executive council, the Directory, both of which were dominated by the upper classes. Paine accordingly returned to the quiet life of a private citizen.

During the next few years, Paine published two of his finest political pamphlets: *The Age of Reason*

The former meeting place of the Jacobins is closed on July 28, 1794. While Paine was in prison, there had been such a conservative reaction to Jacobin rule that by the time of his release France had drifted away from the ideals of republicanism Paine held dear.

and *Agrarian Justice.* Paine began *The Age of Reason* in 1793 and completed the first part in prison. The rise of antireligious movements during the Revolution profoundly disturbed Paine. "The people of France were running headlong into atheism," he said, so he decided to write about his own religious views "lest in the general wreck of superstition, of false systems of government, and false theology, we lose sight of morality, of humanity, and of the theology that is true."

Paine rejected all organized religion, which he maintained was established "to terrify and enslave mankind and monopolize power and profit." "My own mind," he insisted, "is my own church." Paine's religious creed, known as deism, declared that men could discover God within themselves and that serving God simply meant helping one's fellow man. Paine wrote, "I believe in the equality of man; and I believe that religious duties consist in doing justice, loving mercy, and endeavoring to make our fellow-creatures happy."

Paine published the second half of *The Age of Reason* in 1795. While the language of the initial work had been generally moderate and restrained, the new essay resonated with outrage. Paine scathingly attacked each book of the Scriptures and ridiculed the biblical stories of the Garden of Eden, the miracles, and the Virgin Birth as mere fantasy. He bitterly denounced Christianity: "Of all the systems of religion that ever were invented, there is none more derogatory to the Almighty, more unedifying to man, more repugnant to reason, and more contradictory in itself, than this thing called Christianity." Paine insisted that his criticisms in no way impugned the character of Christ. "Jesus Christ was a virtuous and amiable man," he wrote. "The morality he preached and practiced was of the most benevolent kind."

The Age of Reason became an immensely popular and influential work. It presented deist ideas, previously confined to the intelligentsia of the upper classes and the liberal nobility, to a new mass audience. If Paine's political essays radically transformed popular assumptions about politics and

Adam and Eve are driven from the Garden of Eden after succumbing to temptation. In part two of *The Age of Reason*, published in 1795, Paine attacked such biblical stories as mere fantasy, thus alienating the clergy in both Europe and the United States.

Robert Fulton, the inventor of the steam engine, was a frequent visitor at the home of Nicolas de Bonneville, where Paine took up residence in 1797.

society, so too did *The Age of Reason* disrupt the common man's traditional deference to religious institutions. As a consequence, Paine came under a tremendous barrage of criticism from the clergy in Europe and the United States.

Paine wrote *Agrarian Justice* in the winter of 1795–96. The essay was written in the wake of the suppression of the Conspiracy of Equals led by Gracchus Babeuf, a failed radical coup d'état that became known as the first communist movement of the modern era. While Paine wholeheartedly condemned Babeuf's uprising, it nevertheless provoked him to reconsider his own political views. Paine argued that political inequality could not be eradicated so long as economic inequality persisted: He maintained that the first rule of civilization should be "that the condition of every person born into the world, after a state of civilization commences, ought not to be worse than if he had been born before that period."

Paine retreated from Babeuf's radical solution to economic inequality, namely the abolition of private property, for he doubted that an equal distribution of property was either possible or desirable. Yet his denunciation of poverty and human misery was never more passionate or forceful. "The present state of civilization is as odious as it is unjust," he wrote. "It is absolutely the opposite of what it should be, and it is necessary that a revolution should be made in it. The contrast of affluence and wretchedness continually meeting and offending the eye is like dead and living bodies chained together."

In 1797, Paine moved to the home of his close friend Nicolas de Bonneville and lived there for the next six years. Now that he was no longer actively involved in political affairs, Paine could afford to devote his time to more leisurely activities. Paine rarely varied in his easygoing daily routine: He rose late, read the morning newspapers, napped after lunch, took a long walk in the afternoon, and dined with the Bonnevilles. Often, visitors stopped by the Bonneville home to engage Paine in conversation. Lafayette, who returned from exile in 1797, was a frequent guest, as was the American inventor Robert Fulton, the Polish general Tadeusz Kościuszko (who had fought in the American Revolution), and the Irish revolutionary Wolfe Tone. Paine still tinkered with scientific inventions, and he remained obsessed with his iron bridge design. He built a new metal model, and his hammering and pounding at all hours of the night resulted in many sleepless nights for the Bonneville family.

Paine closely monitored the ongoing developments in the French political arena. Although critical of the Directory, he continued to support the French government. Even though democracy had not progressed nearly far enough, Paine still believed that the fundamental accomplishments of the Revolution — the end of the monarchy and feudalism — were worth protecting. Paine accordingly supported the Directory's coup d'état of 1797, which purged from the legislature antirepublican deputies who called for a restoration of the constitutional monarchy. In November 1799, with antirepublican sentiment and rumors of a royalist coup spreading, the five members of the Directory were replaced by

He is vain beyond belief, but he has reason to be vain, and for my part, I forgive him.
—acquaintance of Paine's in London

Thomas Jefferson, inaugurated as U.S. president in March 1801, wrote of Paine that he had "labored, and with as much effect as any man living" to advance "the original sentiments of democracy."

three consuls. The most prominent consul was the charismatic General Napoleon Bonaparte, who had recently returned from his triumphant military campaign in Egypt: Within the year, Napoleon assumed complete control of the government.

Paine had met Napoleon Bonaparte several years earlier when Napoleon was an officer. Surrounded by a huge crowd, Napoleon came to visit Paine at the Bonneville home. With Bonneville acting as an interpreter, Napoleon told Paine that his book *The Rights of Man* had been a tremendous influence and that he even kept a copy of it under his pillow. "A statue of gold," he told Paine, "should be erected to you in every city in the universe." The two men discussed a proposal for the invasion of England that Paine had submitted to the Directory. Although Napoleon would never mount such a campaign, he complimented Paine for his ingenious strategy. Now, three years later, Paine spoke cordially of Napoleon in public, but privately he considered him to be the death knell of the Revolution. At dinner with Joel Barlow, Paine referred to Napoleon as "the greatest butcher of liberty, the greatest monster that nature ever spewed."

After Napoleon's coup, Paine became completely disillusioned with the course of the Revolution, and he longed to return to America, "the country of my heart." He told a close friend, "This is not a country for an honest man to live in; they do not understand anything at all of the principles of free government, and the best way is to leave them to themselves. . . . I know of no Republic in the world except America, which is the only country for such men as you and I." When Thomas Jefferson was inaugurated as president in March 1801, he wrote Paine, offering him passage back to the United States aboard the American warship *Maryland.* Jefferson's letter concluded warmly: "[that] you may long live to continue your useful labors and to reap the reward in the thankfulness of nations is my sincere prayer." Paine declined Jefferson's gracious offer, perhaps still worried about being captured on the open seas by the English navy. Finally, on September 2, 1802, six months after France and England signed a peace treaty, Paine packed his personal papers, bridge models, and belongings and sailed for the United States.

It was more than 25 years since *Common Sense* and *The Crisis* papers had sparked the imagination of the American public. Paine, now 65 years old, would spend the remaining 7 years of his life in quiet obscurity. It was exceedingly difficult for a man such as Paine, who had critically shaped two historic revolutions and almost a third in England, to live outside the familiar spotlight. His writings only appeared in lesser-read journals, his circle of friends grew smaller, and his drinking and temper became more pronounced. In addition, the sickness brought on by his imprisonment finally began to take its toll during these twilight years.

At the time of Paine's arrival in 1802, most people only vaguely recalled his valuable contribution to

Paine spent the last years of his life in the United States in quiet retirement. He was either ignored or ridiculed by American political leaders of the early 1800s, who opposed his deistic religious views.

Thomas Paine's grave site in New Rochelle, New York. As the political tide rose and fell in America and Europe during the tumultuous 18th century, Paine remained true to the ideals of the Enlightenment and devoted his life to attaining them.

the American cause during the War of Independence. His notoriety derived chiefly from his attacks on Christianity in *The Age of Reason* and from a letter of denunciation he had written in France to George Washington, who was venerated by all in America as the father of the country. Paine became embroiled in the partisan political party battles between the Jeffersonian Republicans and the Federalists. Federalist newspapers lampooned Paine as a "loathsome reptile" and a "lying, drunken, brutal infidel" and used his religious views and writings to attack and embarrass Jefferson during the presidential campaign of 1800.

Even many Republicans and old friends, such as Samuel Adams and Benjamin Rush, kept silent and refused to see Paine. Although they strongly supported Paine's views on the French Revolution and republicanism and were even willing to countenance his condemnation of Washington, they vehemently opposed his religious writings. When Jefferson's religious views began to be questioned during the presidential campaign, many Republicans urged Jefferson to distance himself from his friendship with Paine. Jefferson, however, refused to let either the Federalist or the Republican censure affect his cordial relationship with Paine. Paine was a frequent dinner guest at the White House and the two men spent many long hours in conversation about scientific and political issues. They enjoyed an intimate and informal friendship, and Jefferson showed great courage and loyalty in supporting Paine during these troubled times.

Paine spent three months in Washington, D.C., and in February 1803 moved to Bordentown, New Jersey, where he was met by Madame de Bonneville and her three sons (one of the boys, Thomas Paine de Bonneville, was Paine's godson), who had moved to America the previous November. Nicolas de Bonneville had been unable to leave France because of his political activities, and he would arrive in the United States only after Paine's death. Paine took his customary long walks in the afternoon, and each evening he met with friends at the Washington House Tavern. He continued to exchange letters with Jefferson and wrote numerous essays on the political issues of the day, such as the Louisiana Purchase and legal reform in Pennsylvania. His many deist writings were based largely on the arguments in *The Age of Reason*.

Paine returned to his New Rochelle farm, where he stayed for a few years. After the spring of 1806, Paine moved to New York City. His life was now one of "lonely, private misery." Isolated from almost all his old friends and associates, Paine started to drink heavily again, and his health suffered. He worried about his finances constantly in his old age, particularly because of the high cost of medical care.

In the fall of 1808, Paine's health deteriorated sharply. He lost the use of his legs and required constant attention around the clock. Paine convinced Madame de Bonneville to move to Greenwich Village, where the two could share a house and she could look after him. Paine's mental faculties were still active and sharp. "When he could no longer quit his bed, he made some one read the newspapers to him," Madame de Bonneville said. "His mind was always active. He wrote nothing for the press after writing his last will, but he would converse, and took great interest in politics." In March, he applied to a Quaker congregation for permission to be buried in a Quaker cemetery, but his request was denied. In his will, Paine gave the bulk of his estate to Madame de Bonneville, in a trust for the education of her sons. The will ended with these words: "I have lived an honest and useful life; my time has been spent in doing good, and I die in perfect compose and resignation to the will of my creator."

Paine died on June 8, 1809, at eight o'clock in the morning. A funeral service was held in New Rochelle, but only a few people attended, and there was scarcely any public notice about the passing of one of the most celebrated figures of the era. His headstone bore the inscription: "Thomas Paine, author of Common Sense." John Adams, the second president of the United States, had a fitting epitaph: "I know not whether any man in the world has had more influence on its inhabitants or affairs for the last 30 years than Tom Paine."

While he lived, I thought it my duty, as well as a test of my own political principles, to support him against the persecutions of an unprincipled faction.
—THOMAS JEFFERSON

Further Reading

Aldridge, Alfred O. *Man of Reason: The Life of Thomas Paine.* Philadelphia: Lippincott, 1959.

Bailyn, Bernard. *The Ideological Roots of the American Revolution.* Cambridge: Harvard University Press, 1967.

Bruns, Roger. *Thomas Jefferson.* New York: Chelsea House, 1986.

————. *George Washington.* New York: Chelsea House, 1987.

Commager, Henry S. *The Empire of Reason: How Europe Imagined & America Realized the Enlightenment.* New York: Oxford University Press, 1982.

Carson, S. L. *Maximilien Robespierre.* New York: Chelsea House, 1988.

Conway, Moncure D. *Thomas Paine.* 2 vols. 1892. Reprint. New York: Chelsea House, 1983.

Dull, Jonathan R. *A Diplomatic History of the American Revolution.* New Haven: Yale University Press, 1985.

Dwyer, Frank. *Georges Jacques Danton.* New York: Chelsea House, 1987.

Foner, Eric. *Tom Paine and the American Revolution.* New York: Oxford University Press, 1976.

Foote, Michael, and Isaac Kramnick. *The Thomas Paine Reader.* New York: Penguin, 1987.

Hawke, David Freeman. *Paine.* New York: Harper & Row, 1974.

Lancaster, Bruce. *The American Revolution.* Boston: Houghton Mifflin, 1985.

Morris, Richard B. *The Forging of the Union, 1781–1789.* New York: Harper & Row, 1987.

Nevins, Allan, and Henry S. Commager. *Pocket History of the United States.* New York: Washington Square Press, 1982.

Paine, Thomas. *Common Sense.* New York: Penguin, 1982.

————. *Rights of Man.* New York: Penguin, 1984.

Pearson, Hesketh. *Tom Paine: Friend of Mankind.* 1937. Reprint. Philadelphia: Century Bookbindery, 1985.

Schlesinger, Arthur M., jr. *The Birth of a Nation: A Portrait of the American People on the Eve of Revolution.* Boston: Houghton Mifflin, 1988.

Williamson, Audrey. *Thomas Paine: His Life, Work, and Times.* London: Allen & Unwin, 1973.

Chronology

Jan. 29, 1737	Born Thomas Pain (later changed to Paine) in Thetford, England
1750	Leaves grammar school for a three-year apprenticeship at his father's staymaker shop
April 1759	Works as a master staymaker in Sandwich
Sept. 27, 1759	Marries Mary Lambert, who dies before the end of the year
1762–64	Takes job as a supernumery (excise officer)
Aug. 29, 1765	Dismissed from excise post for fraudulent practices; resumes work as staymaker
1766	Teaches English at Goodman's Fields; petitions to be restored to his post as excise officer
1767	Accepts teaching position at Kensington
Feb. 28, 1768	Reappointed to excise post in Lewes
March 26, 1771	Marries Elizabeth Ollive
April 8, 1774	Discharged once more from excise post
Jan. 4, 1759	Parts with his wife, Elizabeth
1774	Sails to Philadelphia and works as a writer and editor
April 17, 1775	The Battle of Lexington begins American revolutionary war
1776	Paine publishes *Common Sense;* enlists in militia and serves in Pennsylvania
Dec. 1776	Begins writing the first *Crisis*
April 1777	Elected to a Committee of Correspondence of the Whig Society of Philadelphia
1778–81	The Deane affair
Feb. 11, 1781	Paine sails to France on the frigate *Alliance;* returns to Boston four months later
Oct. 19, 1781	British surrender at Yorktown, Virginia, effectively ending revolutionary war
1784–85	Paine receives an estate in New Rochelle, New York, and $3,000 as recompense for his wartime services
July 14, 1789	Mob storms Bastille prison, starting French Revolution
1791	Paine publishes *Rights of Man;* sails to France; forms the Republican Society
1793–94	Publishes *Age of Reason;* incarcerated in Luxembourg prison by the French for 10 months
1802	Returns to America
June 8, 1809	Dies in New York City

Index

John Vail is a graduate of the University of Chicago and has received a Ph.D. in political science from Rutgers University. The author of *David Ben-Gurion, Fidel Castro,* and *Nelson and Winnie Mandela* in the Chelsea House series WORLD LEADERS—PAST & PRESENT, he currently resides in Brooklyn, N.Y.

Arthur M. Schlesinger, jr., taught history at Harvard for many years and is currently Albert Schweitzer Professor of the Humanities at City University of New York. He is the author of numerous highly praised works in American history and has twice been awarded the Pulitzer Prize. He served in the White House as special assistant to Presidents Kennedy and Johnson.

PICTURE CREDITS

The Bettmann Archive: pp. 15, 17, 49, 50, 52, 57 (bottom), 58, 59, 64, 65, 66, 74, 77, 81, 83, 84, 87, 88, 89, 92, 97; The Bostonian Society: p. 31; British Museum, Courtesy Norfolk Museums Service (Thetford Museum): p. 98; Culver Pictures: pp. 12, 16, 18, 21, 25, 30, 33 (bottom), 54, 55, 68, 69, 76, 78, 79, 101, 106; The Hulton Deutsch Collection: p. 57 (top); Library of Congress: USZ62-44101, p. 2, USZ62-1550, p. 14, USZ62-2063, p. 26, USZ62-50794, p. 28, USZ62-17110, p. 32, USZ62-50342, p. 33 (top), USZ62-48402, p. 34, USZ62-2140, p. 35, USW33-36626, p. 36, USZ62-93478, p. 37, USZ62-96219, p. 38, USZ62-59097, p. 40, USZ62-5850, p. 41, USZ62-39584, p. 42, USZ62-26779, p. 43, USZ62-5010, p. 44, USZ62-24644, p. 45, USZ62-9578, p. 46, USZ62-1217, p. 56, USZ62-10833, p. 60, USZ62-69473, p. 61, USZ62-46915, p. 62, USZ62-10967, p. 67, USZ62-13460, p. 72, p. 80, USZ62-17334, p. 82, USZ62-5889, p. 90, USZ62-1896, p. 94, 31184, p. 95, p. 100, USZ62-20996, p. 102, USZ62-21602, p. 104, USZ62-21932, p. 105; Mary Evans Picture Library: pp. 24, 70, 71; National Maritime Museum, p. 22; Norfolk Museum Service (Thetford Museum): p. 73